HOW TO
SPEC
AND BUY
TYPE

A precise guide to the art of copyfitting.

To my wife Ann
A perfect example of the student surpassing the teacher

HOW TO SPEC AND BUY TYPE

A precise guide to the art of copyfitting.

by TOM CARDAMONE

Designed and Illustrated by Ann Cardamone

Art Direction Book Company • New York

ISBN: 0-88108-049-7 (Cloth)
        0-88108-050-0 (Paper)

Library of Congress Catalog Card Number: 88–70437

Published by Art Direction Book Company
            10 East 39th Street
            New York, New York 10016

Table of Contents

Introduction

"Can you spec type?" I doubt there is an artist in advertising or publishing who hasn't been asked that question at one time or another.

There is one thing I've noticed about professional artists—many of us seem to have forgotten there was a time when we did not know our craft. The art director who tells you that type speccing is "very easy" has forgotten that there was a time when he/she didn't even know what "type speccing" (pronounced "specking") meant.

If type specifying is so simple, then why has it taken me (as well as my fellow artists who work with type) so long to learn it well enough to be trusted? The fact is that the formula itself is quite simple. It does, however, take a fair amount of diversified experience to develop the in-depth understanding necessary for its application.

The reason I have written this book is that I have finally given in to so many requests from my students and fellow artists. We have all wished that there had been a book like this available when we were learning.

Oddly enough, there are many excellent reference books on typography. But most concentrate on designing with type, its history, and methods of setting type. Very little space, usually no more than four or five pages of an entire text, is devoted to how to specify or order type. They adequately explain the principle and formula for specifying type, but then stop, leaving the reader unaware of all the requirements.

Professional art directors with a broad variety of type specification experiences can order typography with a complete understanding of an anticipated result. Their experiences encompass layout problems other than a block of text to fit a designated area. It goes beyond setting "flush left" and/or right. They can mark up a complicated tabular layout for an annual report so explicitly that the typographer will create precisely what is designated to fit the layout. They can spec a brochure with heads, subheads and run-arounds to fit the layout or specify a manuscript for a complicated textbook. *They can anticipate problems before the type has been set* and have the expertise necessary to make the copy and the layout work.

All this has nothing to do with type *design*. I am referring to the mechanics, the limitations and boundaries, the peculiarities of type as an element. It is very much like choosing a kind of brick to build a building. The brick is only one aspect of the project. Getting it to physically work with the architecture is quite another challenge. The type face is a matter of design preference; personal or otherwise. Specifying precisely what you want the typesetter to produce is an acquired skill.

Type specification is truly indispensable. It is a craft necessary to the production of printed matter. Once the formula and academic principles are understood, it may take time to perfect. The reason it often takes longer to learn than you might expect has to do with exposure. Not all art departments have the scope of type setting problems necessary to acquire the experience. Working for a number of different companies might be what it takes.

Please don't ever forget that type design and type specification are integrated efforts. Type specification instructs a typographer to set type according to your design. First you choose a type face (style); then you design with it. Your design is either in your head or in layout form. Then, when you feel you know what you want to achieve, you order type to be set in a certain way. That is what this book is about. *How to tell the typographer what you want.*

Because there are so many good books on type, typography, and designing with type, we will focus upon *ordering* type. You may be surprised to learn how much more you can accomplish as an art director once you become proficient at ordering type.

I hope this book will help you say someday,
"Type speccing? It's easy."

7

Chapter One
A New Language

Computerized typesetting. A boon to the world of communication. If Gutenberg were alive today he would not only be proud to know that he started it all, he would also be mesmerized by its technology. And rightfully so. Typography has advanced so rapidly during the past decade that it is difficult to keep abreast of its ever changing progress.

We are currently in the midst of a typography renaissance. New equipment is constantly being introduced and new type shops are opening throughout the country. In addition, advertising agencies and corporations are installing their own typesetting systems.

This is what you hear from the computer typesetting world: "This system can do everything! It can stretch, shrink, twist, mix faces and sizes, condense, expand, enlarge, reduce, run around, make corrections, automatically hyphenate, justify, incorporate halftones. . . ." And it is all true. There is, however, one thing that is being glossed over. Someone still has to tell the operator what to do in order to set the type the way you want it. Someone has to specify the code necessary to do it all. Here is what takes place in the process of typesetting. Compare it with the past, when type was set using the linotype method.

You, as the designer, would indicate what you wanted the typographer to set using a system of symbols and terms derived from the operational procedure of the equipment used. For example, "leading" is a term used for controlling the line space between lines. A sliver of lead was inserted between each line of type creating a different line spacing – or "leading." The term is still used to some degree today, although it is no longer done that way. Now we simply call it "line spacing." When the typesetter received a marked up manuscript the specifications were read as actual directions for him to follow in operating the equipment. The end result: what you specified was what you got!

Because this system of setting type in metal had physical limitations, the designer relied heavily on mechanical paste up methods to refine the typography. Type specifying wasn't particularly difficult but nevertheless required a fair amount of know-how.

Typesetting today offers a universe of possibilities. As a result of this, mechanical preparation has been greatly simplified. Much of what was done in a "mechanical" can now be done by the typesetting system. While there may be less to do in the mechanical stage, the *designer* must now do and know *more* to make this possible. You must literally "describe" a mechanical layout to the typesetter using symbols and terms. *This means you must know more about ordering type now than ever before.*

If you want something set to a particular shape or in

a specific position you must know how to specify it in order to avoid a complicated mechanical. This can only be done with the knowledge of type specifying, layout methods and terminology. Knowing how to mark up a manuscript is more involved today, and infinitely more important.

Your marked up copy is not necessarily given directly to an operator. It is usually intercepted by a "type specifier" who must translate your specifications into the code that the operator needs to program his typesetting system. Your mark up has to be precise or it will be incorrectly translated.

Pica... face... descender... open... lead... extended... serif... the terms, names, and expressions used in typography could fill a book.

The more you use a language the more articulate you will become. So it is with the typographer's language. It must be used regularly in order for it to become your most valuable tool as an art director. That's why the terms are in this first chapter, where they belong, rather in the back of the book. My advice is to take some time now to study them before continuing to the next chapter. Then constantly refer to them as you progress through the text. Note that in addition to the terminology itself there are specific symbols called "proofreaders' marks" used to designate much of it.

TERMS OF THE TYPOGRAPHER

AA (Author's Alterations)
This is a polite way of referring to a customer's changes after the type has been set.

Agate
Many newspapers and some magazines measure the *depth* of their text columns in terms of the number of lines of type. The standard measurement is called "Agate," which can be found on an "Agate" ruler. Fourteen agates equal one inch. The column *width* may vary according to the publication and is measured in inches or picas (see PICA).

Ascender
The upper stroke in small letters of the alphabet, as in the letter "b."

Body Copy
That portion of type which constitutes the main part of the text as opposed to the headings. For example:

Heading   **A NEW LANGUAGE**

           The more you use a language the more articulate you will become. So it is with the typographer's lan-
Body copy   guage. It must be used regularly in order for it to become your most valuable tool as an art director.

Bold Face Type
Type that is *darker* in contrast to another with which it is used.

Caps (and Small Caps)
Two sizes of capital letters in one size of a type alphabet, i.e. SMALL CAPS. The small capitals are approximately the size of the lower case letters.

Characters
Letter forms are referred to as characters.

Cold Type
A method of printing type from hand operated machinery such as the typewriter or word processing systems. Also referred to as "strike-on" type.

Color
A portion of type such as a column or a headline in itself creates a visual tonality called "color." A paragraph of bold-face type will appear darker in color than a paragraph of light type. A light type headline will appear lighter in color than a bold headline, i.e.

THIS HEADLINE IS LIGHT IN COLOR

A portion of type such as a column or a headline in itself creates a visual tonality called "color." A paragraph of bold-face type will appear darker in color than a paragraph of light type. A light type headline will appear lighter in color than a bold headline.

THIS HEADLINE IS DARKER IN COLOR

A portion of type such as a column or a headline in itself creates a visual tonality called "color." A paragraph of bold-face type will appear darker in color than a paragraph of light type. A light type headline will appear lighter in color than a bold headline.

Composition
The setting of type. The place where type is set is called a "composing room." The person who sets the type is called the "compositor." However, "compositor" seems to be used in publishing firms, whereas the title "typographer" is more commonly used in advertising.

Condensed

A style of type that is narrow or slender as compared with normal type, i.e.

NORMAL TYPE　　CONDENSED TYPE

Copy

The original material to be converted into type.

Copy Fitting

The act of determining a specific type face (see FACE) and size to fit a given area. Seems to have been replaced by the term "type specifying," "type specification," "type speccing," and "casting off."

Delete

To remove.

Descender

The stroke below the body of the small letters as in the letter "g" or "y."

Display Type

Type that is larger than the text. Headline type. The type used in this book to identify the chapter titles is display type.

Ellipsis

Three dots in a row...

em

The square of a particular type size. Usually associated with the letter "m."

en

One-half the width of an em.

Extended Type

A type style that is wide or stretched as compared with normal type, i.e.

NORMAL TYPE

EXTENDED TYPE

Face

The style, configuration or design of an alphabet. Each face has its own name. The name of the text type in this book is called "Century Expanded."

Flush

The vertical alignment of type along its left or right edge (or both).

FLUSH LEFT	The vertical alignment of type along its left edge.	The vertical alignment of type along its right edge.	FLUSH RIGHT

Flush Paragraph

A paragraph with no indentation.

FLUSH PARAGRAPH	This paragraph of text is a flush paragraph because the first line does not indent.
INDENTED PARAGRAPH	This paragraph of text is an indented paragraph because the first line is indented.

Folio

Page number.

Font

The complete assortment of type in one size and style, i.e.

New Century Schoolbook Black Italic

abcdefghijklmnopqrstuvwxyz
ABCDEFGHIJKLMNOPQRSTUVW
XYZ1234567890 .,;:&!?$*

Format

The layout to be used for a printed piece. Or the overall shape and arrangement of a type group.

Glassine

A type setting on thin translucent paper or clear acetate used to make rough layouts or simply to check against a layout.

Hot Metal

Type that is cast and set either by hand or machine from a melted lead and tin composition.

Italic

A style of letter formation that slants forward (*to the right*).

THIS IS ITALIC

Justify

To space out a line or lines of type to a uniform or designated width. Also referred to as flush left and right.

When all the lines of a paragraph are equal in length and are flush left and flush right it is referred to as "justified."

Kerning

In photo typesetting, closing the space between characters, i.e.

This is normal letter spacing.
This is kerned letter spacing.

Lead (Leading) pronounced "LED"

In machine or metal typesetting, a thin strip of lead used for adding or adjusting the space between lines of type. Its thickness is measured in points.

Leaders

Rows of dots or dashes used in tables, programs, etc., i.e.

Letterspacing

Opening or adding space between each character (letter) of a word.

This is normal letterspacing.
T h i s   i s   l e t t e r   s p a c e d .

Light Face

A type face that is light in weight (color) as compared with others.

Logotype (Logo/Trademark)

The name of a product or company in a special design used to establish exclusive identity. Also known as a trademark. Although a trademark does not necessarily spell out the name—it might only be initials or a symbol, i.e.

Lower Case

The small letters of an alphabet as opposed to the CAPITAL letters. The expression was derived from the method of handsetting type. The alphabet consists of individual metal letters which are stored in wooden cases. One case of the capital letters, another case for the small letters. When in use they are positioned on a table one above the other, the *upper* case containing capitals, the *lower* case containing small letters.

Mark Up

The term used to define your written specifications.

Measure

The width of a word, headline or line of type.

PE

Printer's error.

Pica

A standard unit of measurement used to determine the width or depth of type. There are approximately 6 picas to an inch.

0 1 2 3 4 5 6 Picas

1 Inch

Point

Also a standard unit of measurement used to designate type sizes. There are 12 points to a pica. Approximately 72 points to an inch.

Rag

Type that is not lined up vertically along one edge or both.

	Type that is not	
FLUSH	lined up	RAG
LEFT	vertically along	RIGHT
	one edge or	
	both.	

Reader's Proof

A preliminary setting on inexpensive paper for layout and proofreading purposes.

Reproduction Proof (Repro Proof; see Type Proof)

The final typesetting produced on special paper to be used in the preparation of mechanicals for reproduction.

Roman

The normal configuration of a letter consisting of a vertical stroke as opposed to an italic (slanted), i.e.

THIS IS ROMAN
THIS IS ITALIC

Run-around

Setting type in such a manner that it fits around a picture or particular shape.

Run-In

Copy that is to continue without a paragraph break.

Running Head

The title of a book or magazine appearing at the top of each page.

Running Foot

The title (or such information) at the bottom of each page.

Serif
The short cross line on a letter in certain type faces, i.e.

ABCDEF
abcdefghi

Serif

Type faces without serifs are called "sans serif," i.e.

ABCDEF
abcdefgh

Stet
A word used to indicate to the typographer or proofreader to ignore an indicated correction and let it remain as it was.

Template
A layout establishing a specific format or arrangement to be followed in setting type.

Text
Same as "body copy."

Transpose
To change the position of a character, word or line of type with another character, word or line, i.e. W R O D - W O R D. The O and R were transposed.

Turnover ("TO")
Copy that runs beyond a designated width and must be continued on the next line.

Copy that runs beyond a designated width and must be continued on the next line.

Turnover

Type Gauge
A ruler calibrated in picas, points and/or agates used in measuring type.

Type Proof (Galley)
The paper on which the set type is produced.

Upper Case
Capital letters.

Widow
A single word or hyphenated portion of a word in a line by itself, at the end of a paragraph. *Ugly!*

PROOFREADERS' MARKS

The following proofreaders' marks are standard and must be memorized. It will take considerable practice and experience to learn how to use them. You will realize soon enough how indispensable they are.

The three columns below explain the use of each mark. Column One is the actual mark with its definition beside it. Column Two is the mark as it would be used. Column

Three is the result of the marking. Also note that in some instances a combination of two marks is used, one in the margin and a corresponding mark in the text to indicate where the change is to be made.

You cannot specify type if you do not know how to use these symbols.

TYPE SPECIFICATION SYMBOLS AND PROOFREADERS' MARKS

Symbol & Definition		Application	Typeset Result
> ∧	"Caret" used to indicate where a change is to be inserted		
ℓ	Delete or take out	Now is the time and place ℓ	Now is the time
( ) ⌒	Close up; take out space or delete and close up	Now is the time and place	Now is the time and place

TYPE SPECIFICATION SYMBOLS AND PROOFREADERS' MARKS

Symbol & Definition		Application	Typeset Result
$+ \#$	Insert (more) space	$+ \#$ Now is the time	Now is the time
		$+ \#$ Now is the time and the place	Now is the time and the place
$- \#$	or Take out space	$- \#$ Now is the time and the place	Now is the time and the place
☐	One em (quad) indent	☐ Now is the time to learn these marks	Now is the time to learn these marks
		☐ Now is the time to learn these marks	Now is the time to learn these marks
◻	One en (or one half em) indent	◻ Now is the time to learn these marks	Now is the time to learn these marks
Stet	Ignore indicated change. Let it remain as it was	Now is the time to learn these marks *Stet*	Now is the time to learn these marks
⊙	Period	Now is the time ⊙	Now is the time.
⋀	Comma	Now for sure is the time.	Now, for sure, is the time.
⋀;	Semicolon	Now is the time the time is now.	Now is the time; the time is now.
⊙:	Colon	Now is the time	Now is the time:
⋁	Apostrophe or single quote	Now is the time.	'Now is the time.'
⋁	Open quote	Now is the time.	"Now is the time.
⋁	Close quote	"Now is the time.	"Now is the time."
?/	Question mark	Now is the time ?	Now is the time?
!/	Exclamation point	Now is the time !	Now is the time!
=	Hyphen	Now is the time	Now-is-the-time
⊄ ⊅	Parenthesis	Now is the time	(Now is the time)
$\frac{\mid}{M}$	Dash (one em)	Now is the time $\frac{\mid}{M}$	Now is the time —
◯ *wf*	Wrong font or type face	Now is (the time) *wf*	Now is the time
/ or *lc*	Set in lower case	Now is (THE TIME) *lc*	Now is the time
		Now is THE TIME	now is the time
≡	Set in caps	Now the time	Now is the TIME
≡ ⌐	Set in lower case with initial caps	NOW IS THE TIME	Now Is The Time

TYPE SPECIFICATION SYMBOLS AND PROOFREADERS' MARKS

Symbol & Definition		Application	Typeset Result
═══	Set in small caps	Now is the time	NOW is the TIME
──	Set in italics	Now is the time	*Now is the time*
rom	Set in roman type	rom Now is the time rom	Now is the time
lf	Set in light face	Now is the time lf	Now is the time
～～～	Set in bold face	Now is the time	**Now** is the **time**
～～～ (double)	Set in bold face italics	Now is the time	Now is the ***time***
≈≈≈	Set in bold face caps	Now is the time	Now is the **TIME**
⌐	Move to the right	Now ▭ is the time Now ⌐ is the time	Now is the time
⌐ (left)	Move to the left	▭ Now is the time ⌐Now is the time	Now is the time
⊔ ⌐ ⌐	Center within a given space	Now is the time	Now is the time
│	Centered lines or words	Now is the time Now is the time	Now is the time Now is the time
⊔	Lower	Now is the time	Now is the time
⊓	Raise	Now is the time	Now is the time
══	Align horizontally	Now is the time	Now is the time
‖	Align vertically (flush)	⌐ Now ⌐ is the time Now is the time	Now is the time
¶	Begin a paragraph	¶ Now is the time and the place to learn these marks.	Now is the time and the place to learn these marks

TYPE SPECIFICATION SYMBOLS AND PROOFREADERS' MARKS

	Symbol & Definition	Application	Typeset Result
	No paragraph. Let copy run in	Now, for sure, is the time to learn these marks. This is the place.	Now, for sure, is the time to learn these marks. This is the place.
⊏ or ‖	No paragraph indent	Now is the time and the place to learn these marks.	Now is the time and the place to learn these marks.
tr ∿	Transpose	Now is teh time and place the	Now is the time and the place
⌐	End (break) line here	Now, for sure, is the time and the place to learn these marks.	Now, for sure, is the time and the place to learn these marks.
⟨···⟩	Ellipsis or tri-dot	Now is the time ···	Now is the time…
✕	Fix (broken type)	✕ Now is the time	Now is the time
◯ DNS	Do not set	Now is the time DNS	

TYPE SETTING METHODS

For the sake of simplification I will not go into any great detail on the subject of typesetting methods. While to some degree it is important to know them, it is not essential to learning type specification. However, those aspects of type setting that affect type specification will be discussed throughout the text.

The following is a synopsis of the major typesetting methods. They should not be interpreted to be as simple as their description because they are indeed more intricate. Further information should be pursued.

Hand Set

Handsetting involves the setting of individual metal "slugs" each containing one character, punctuation, numeral or symbol. The type is assembled and placed into form, inked and printed onto a sheet of paper called a type proof.

Hand set type is primarily used for setting headlines or large display type faces. It is rarely, if ever, used for text. *The system itself has, for the most part, been replaced by photography.*

Machine Set

The machine method of setting type that seems to be surviving the typography revolution is called "linotype." It sets a one piece metal slug containing a complete line of type and is used primarily for text. Linotype is referred to as "machine" type as well as "hot metal" because each line is actually cast by machine from a molten lead and tin combination. *This method will soon be all but replaced by phototypography.*

Phototypography

Setting type by computerized, photographic systems, is of course the most modern and efficient method. The type is set precisely as the name implies – photographically. The characters are individually photographed and composed onto a film negative and photocopied onto white photopaper which is also called a "type proof" or "print out."

In phototypography there is virtually no limit to the size of type, small or large. It is generally used for both text and headlines and is rapidly replacing the machine methods.

The number and variety of photographic type setting systems is so vast and has become so sophisticated it is mind boggling.

Cold Type

This relatively inexpensive method sets type using a keyboard that strikes the individual character directly against the paper as does the ordinary typewriter. This is also called "strike-on" type.

Due to the fact that phototypography is predominant in the industry, this text will be geared toward specifying photo type. Occasional reference may be made to the other methods.

Fig. 1

Chapter Two
Tools and Rules

THE TYPE GAUGE

There are several styles of type gauges available in the average art supply store, any one of which is suitable. Some display only pica and agate measurements while others are calibrated in picas, points, agates and inches.

One very easy-to-use gauge is the Haberule© It is calibrated in points, picas and inches on both sides. Note that the 12 point column is also picas; Fig. 1.

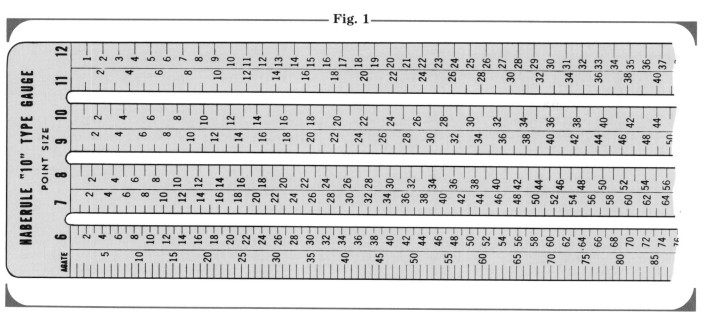

THE TYPE SPECIMEN BOOK

Most good typographers will provide their customers with a book or catalog which displays all of their available type styles. It might show a complete font for each type face in only one size or it may illustrate a paragraph setting in several sizes and line spacings. This will vary from book to book.

It should also contain a *character count* table or chart section, listing the number of characters per pica for each face in its available sizes. Without such a book type specification is practically impossible. Its use will be described shortly but first a word of caution.

Due to the fact that type faces of the same name will vary slightly from one manufacturer to the next it is advisable to avoid mixing type shops on matching portions of the same job unless they have the same equipment. Mixing type shops in this manner could result in a variation in type color, paragraph depth, line breaks and so on. Consult your typographer in these situations.

THE FORMULA

Any type specification project consists of the following categories: The Problem; Calculation; Specifications; End Result.

The Problem is a combination of the manuscript or copy to be set and the area (layout) it is to occupy when set in type.

Calculation is the application of the formula to determine the type face and size into which the copy is to be converted.

Specifications are the actual written instructions to the typesetter, detailing precisely how you want the type to be set.

End Result is the final type setting as you specified it.

The formula used in type calculation is quite simple, consisting of only two functions. One is to define the area to be occupied by a sentence or paragraph. The other is to determine the length of a word or line of words when converted into type.

Let's take it one step at a time following the two functions outlined above. *It is advisable that you actually perform the exercises* described in the text as you read along in order to maximize your understanding. A simple but good calculator will be extremely helpful. The main purpose of the formula is to determine the area to be occupied by the text copy. It is similar to determining the square footage of a given area. You would multiply the length by the width. For example, a room 10 feet wide by 9 feet long would have an area of 90 square feet (10 × 9 = 90).

If you planned on laying tiles on your kitchen floor and wanted to determine how many tiles you needed, you would count the number of tiles that fill the *width* in one row by the number of tiles that would fill the *length* in one

row. So that if the tiles were on foot square you would multiply 10 tiles wide by 9 tiles long to equal a total of 90 tiles. It's the same as saying 9 rows of 10 tiles.

If the tiles were smaller in size, say 6 inches square, you would get 20 tiles across the width (10 feet wide equals 120 total inches divided by 6 inches equals 20 tiles). The length is 9 feet converted to inches equals 108 total inches divided by 6 inches equals 18 tiles. To find the total number of tiles for the area multiply 20 by 18 to equal 360 tiles. This is your formula; Fig. 2. Let's apply it to a given problem.

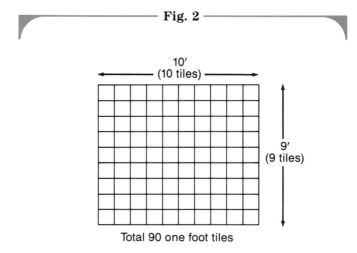

— **Fig. 2** —

10′
(10 tiles)

9′
(9 tiles)

Total 90 one foot tiles

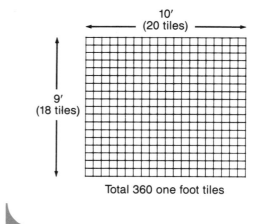

10′
(20 tiles)

9′
(18 tiles)

Total 360 one foot tiles

The Problem

You have a layout area that measures 18 picas wide by 6 picas deep. The copy to be converted into type for that area is in Fig. 3. The problem is what size type will fit that area?

Calculation

The first thing you need to know is the *total number of characters* there are in the copy. The formula is the same as in determining the number of tiles in a given area.

Step One—Count the number of characters across one line. Don't forget the punctuation and spaces between words. Because the copy you will work with is usually type-

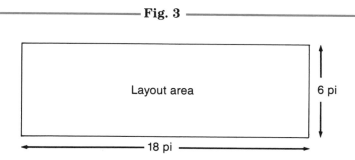

Fig. 3

Layout area

6 pi

18 pi

Type specifying is a skill to be learned in progressive levels each of which supports the other. Each exercise in this text is based upon information learned in the previous exercise, getting more intricate as it continues. If you skip pages or sections you will be directly opposing its structure. It is no different than learning any other skill. You wouldn't skip chapters or exercises in a math book, for example.

Copy

written, the line length will vary. Rule a light vertical pencil line through the copy at a point that appears to be the *average length* of line containing the least number of capitals (or none). Count the characters in that line; Fig. 4.

Fig. 4

Type specifying is a skill to be learned in progressive levels each of which supports the other.) 51 characters
Each exercise in this text is based upon information learned in the previous exercise, getting more intricate as it continues. If you skip pages or sections you will be directly opposing its structure. It is no different than learning any other skill. You wouldn't skip chapters or exercises in a math book, for example.

Step Two – Count the number of average lines (7) and multiply it by 51 to equal a total number of characters (357).

Step Three – Count the characters to the right of the vertical line, including the space at the *end* of each line as well as the last line for a total of 71. Add 71 to 357 for a final total of 428 characters; Fig. 5.

Fig. 5

Type specifying is a skill to be learned in

progressive levels each of which supports the other."

Each exercise in this text is based upon information"

learned in the previous exercise, getting more intricate'

as it continues. If you skip pages or sections you'will'

be directly opposing its structure. It is no different'

than learning any other skill. You wouldn't skip chapters'

or exercises in a math book, for example.

$$\begin{array}{r} 30 \\ 41 \\ \hline 71 \\ 357 \\ \hline 428 \end{array}$$

30 *characters*

41 *characters*

Fig. 2 demonstrates that the size of the tile determines the number of tiles that would fill the space. The smaller the tiles, the more will fit. The larger the tile, the fewer will fit. So it is with type. The size of the type will determine how much will fit a given area.

Our layout measures 18 pi × 6 pi*. We have estimated that we have 428 characters to fill the space. Will they fit?

Step Four – Select a type face and size you want to use. You will not know if it will fit until it has been calculated.

Let's use Century Textbook Bold as shown in Fig. 6A. and select 9 point for the size.

Refer to the table in Fig. 6B. Find "9" (point) in the row across the top. Read down that column to where it aligns with your selected typeface (Century Textbook Bold) and you have the number of characters per pica (2.70). Multiply 2.70 by the pica width of the layout (18) to equal 48.60 characters. This means that 48.60 characters will fill one line 18 picas wide. You need to know how many lines 428 characters will occupy.

Step Five – Divide 48.60 into 428 to equal 8.81. This means 8 full lines plus 81% of another line.

When working with type each line is considered to be a line whether it is a full or short line. Therefore the fraction is to be considered a line. The answer is 9 lines.

Step Six – You have calculated that 428 characters of 9 point type set on an 18 pica measure will run 9 lines deep. Question: how deep is 9 lines?

When text is set, it is done with a standard space between lines. This is called "set solid." Line spacing can be varied to accommodate a layout, but for the time being we will base our calculation on a solid setting.

Now take your type gauge and locate the "9" in the *9 point column*. This indicates the depth of *9 lines* of 9 point. Place the gauge on your layout to see how it compares with the 6 pica depth. *Note that it is too deep*; Fig. 7.

Step Seven – If 9 point is too large you will have to recalculate using a smaller size. Let's try 8 point. Refer back to the table in Fig. 6b and note that 8 point Century Textbook Bold is 3.05 characters per pica. Multiply 3.05 by 18 to equal 54.90 characters per line. Divide 54.90 into 428 to equal 7.80 lines or 8 full lines of 8 point type.

Step Eight – Using the 8 point slot on your gauge, measure 8 lines against the layout. Note that it will fall slightly short of the 6 picas, *but it will fit!* The 6 picas in this instance is only a maximum depth, not an absolute. We will return to this later in the text (See page 25).

So much for CALCULATION.

---

*As a general rule, when dimensions are indicated, the width is usually the first figure and the letter "x" is used to represent the word "by" or "on" followed by the height or depth. 18 pi W × 6 pi D.

---- Fig. 6A ----

ABCDEFGHIJKLMNOPQRSTUVW
XYZ&abcdefghijklmnopqrstuvwxyz
ÇÑçéıñßfifffffiflffl
1234567890
(.,:;"'*¿?¡!)%¢$/£

TASTE IN PRINTING DETERMINES THE FO rm typography is to take. The selection of a congruo us typeface, the quality and the suitability for its pu rpose of the paper being used, the care and labor, time and cost of the materials devoted to its production, all in a direct ratio to its ultimate worth and destination

Century Textbook Bold

---- Fig. 6B ----

TYPEFACE NAME

CHARACTER PER PICA

	6	7	8	9	10	11	12	14	18	24	30	36	48	60	72
Century Textbook D	—	—	—	—	—	—	—	1.87	1.45	1.09	.87	.73	.54	.44	.36
Century Textbook Italic T	4.08	3.48	3.05	2.70	2.44	2.23	2.04	1.74	1.35	1.02	—	—	—	—	—
Century Textbook Italic D	—	—	—	—	—	—	—	1.87	1.45	1.09	.87	.73	.54	.44	.36
Century Textbook Bold T	4.08	3.48	3.05	2.70	2.44	2.23	2.04	1.74	1.35	1.02	—	—	—	—	—
Century Textbook Bold D	—	—	—	—	—	—	—	1.70	1.32	.99	.79	.66	.50	.40	.33
Century Light (ITC) T/D	4.35	3.73	3.27	2.90	2.61	2.38	2.18	1.86	1.45	1.09	.87	.73	.54	.44	.36
Century Light Italic (ITC) T/D	4.31	3.69	3.23	2.87	2.58	2.35	2.15	1.84	1.43	1.08	.86	.72	.54	.43	.36
Century Book (ITC) T/D	4.12	3.53	3.09	2.74	2.47	2.24	2.06	1.76	1.37	1.03	.82	.69	.51	.41	.34
Century Book Italic (ITC) T/D	4.09	3.51	3.07	2.73	2.46	2.23	2.05	1.75	1.36	1.02	.82	.68	.51	.41	.34
Century Bold (ITC) T/D	3.83	3.29	2.87	2.56	2.30	2.09	1.92	1.64	1.28	.96	.77	.64	.48	.38	.32
Century Bold Italic (ITC) T/D	3.86	3.31	2.90	2.58	2.32	2.11	1.93	1.66	1.29	.97	.77	.64	.48	.39	.32
Century Ultra (ITC) T/D	3.06	2.63	2.30	2.04	1.84	1.67	1.53	1.31	1.02	.77	.61	.51	.38	.31	.26
Century Ultra Italic (ITC) T/D	3.05	2.61	2.29	2.03	1.83	1.66	1.53	1.31	1.02	.76	.61	.51	.38	.30	.25
Century Light Condensed (ITC) T/D	5.25	4.49	3.93	3.50	3.15	2.86	2.62	2.25	1.75	1.31	1.05	.87	.66	.52	.44
Century Light Condensed Italic (ITC) T/D	5.16	4.42	3.90	3.44	3.09	2.81	2.58	2.21	1.72	1.29	1.03	.86	.64	.52	.43
Century Book Condensed (ITC) T/D	5.09	4.36	3.82	3.39	3.05	2.76	2.54	2.18	1.70	1.27	1.02	.85	.64	.51	.42
Century Book Condensed Italic (ITC) T/D	4.88	4.18	3.67	3.25	2.93	2.66	2.44	2.09	1.63	1.22	.98	.81	.61	.49	.41
Century Bold Condensed (ITC) T/D	4.67	4.00	3.50	3.11	2.80	2.55	2.34	2.00	1.56	1.17	.93	.78	.58	.47	.39
Century Bold Condensed Italic (ITC) T/D	4.69	4.02	3.52	3.13	2.81	2.56	2.35	2.01	1.56	1.17	.94	.78	.59	.47	.39

---- Fig. 7 ----

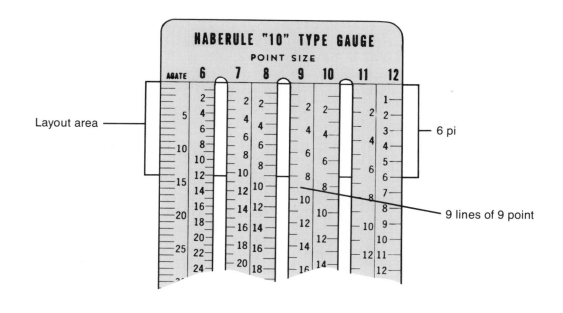

Layout area

HABERULE "10" TYPE GAUGE

6 pi

9 lines of 9 point

Specifications

You concluded that 8 point Century Textbook Bold, set × 18 picas will fit the layout. When you mark up the manuscript the specifications are actually a literal description of what the end result should look like. Until now we have been concerned with the overall depth and width—not the format of the type block. We want the text to be set flush left and right (justified) with no paragraph indent. It is also to be set solid in 8 point. This is indicated as "$\frac{8}{8}$ pt."

With these specifications in mind, take a look at the marked up copy in Fig. 8. Note the indication for c/lc which is short for caps and lower case.

When you write your specifications it is advisable to use a colored pencil which will make it easier for the typographer to read. Avoid light, pastel colors for this. It is a strain on the typographer. Use a graphite pencil, or red or *dark* blue pencil. Now there are two schools of thought regarding pencil vs ink or felt pen. On a simple spec with a slight chance that you will change it, you can use ink or felt pen. But on a complicated markup, changes could be frequent. If you use ink or Pentel you'll be forced to scratch and cross out, creating a mess. If pencil is used you can erase it and keep it neat. I cannot overemphasize the importance of a neat, orderly, legible mark up. We are inclined to forget that what we order must also be paid for. If it is wrong it could be quite costly in time as well as money. The type operator must read and interpret your instructions. When you write specifications you are literally describing a layout. Make it perfectly clear!

That's it. That is the formula. It is reasonably simple in principle and appears to be all there is to it. However, this mathematical procedure is just the tool. The layout and editorial requirements are what make its application challenging. This will become apparent as we progress. For example, note the indication for no paragraph indent and transposition of copy in Fig. 8. If you had neglected to indicate it the setting would have been incorrect and would have to be reset—this would be considered an AA.

Fig. 8

$\frac{8}{8}$ PT. *Century Textbook Bold*
c/lc   Flush l/r × 18 picas

Type specifying is a skill to be learned in

progressive levels each of which supports the other.

Each exercise in this text is based upon information

learned in the previous exercise, getting more intricate

as it continues. If you skip pages or sections you will

be directly opposing its structure. It is no different

than learning any other skill. You wouldn't skip chapters

or exercises in a math book for example.

End Result

Fig. 9

6 pi

Type specifying is a skill to be learned in progressive levels each of which supports the other. Each exercise in this text is based upon information learned in the previous exercise, getting more intricate as it continues. If you skip pages or sections you will be directly opposing its structure. It is no different than learning any other skill. For example, you wouldn't skip chapters or exercises in a math book.

So much for setting a simple block of text. Now let's investigate the other function of calculation which is to determine the length of a word or line of words as in a sub-headline or caption.

The Problem

You must set a simple four word line of copy (in caps and lower case) that reads: Set this in type!

The maximum length (or width) permitted in the layout is 12 picas. This is called the "measure."

Calculation

Step One—Count the number of characters in the copy. Once more, when counting characters you must count the *space between words* as well as the actual characters and punctuation. Set this in type! contains 17 characters. Count them.

Step Two—Select a type face and size. We'll use the same face but a larger size, say 24 point. Locate 24 at the top of the table in Fig. 6b and read down to the Century Textbook Bold row (1.02 characters per pica). Divide 1.02 into 17 characters (16.67 picas). This means that 24 pt. will run longer than 16 picas. Eventually your eye will be sufficiently trained to know that 24 pt. is too large. Try a smaller size.

Take particular notice that the sizes shown are not in continuous numerical sequence. This simply means that these are the only sizes available. There is no 22 point for instance. So let's try the 18 point column. This shows 1.35 characters per pica, which when divided into 17, equals 12.59 picas. This seems reasonably close enough. However the consideration here is how strictly we must adhere to the 12 picas. If it is only a rough size, then we can set it in 18 point. If it is an absolute maximum width, then we must try the next smaller size, which is 14 point. You can tell without calculation that is is going to be much smaller than you would prefer.

You could take the chance and have it set in 18 point. There is a possibility that it may not run wider than 12 picas. After all one of the characters is a punctuation mark, there are two "i"s and three "t"s, and you could always photostat it down to 12 picas. Let's take the chance.

Specifications

You have concluded that 18 pt. Century Textbook Bold in cap and lower case is what you want. This is exactly what you should write on the copy to be sent to the typographer.

If the original copy has been typed in cap and lower case, indicate your specifications as in Fig. 10A.

If it is typed in all caps use the symbol for cap, lower case and bold face as shown in Fig. 10B.

Fig. 10

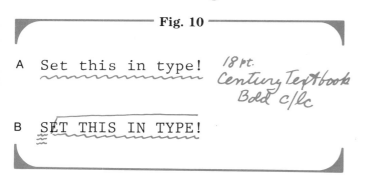

End Result

Fig. 11

Set this in type!

|← 12 picas →|

It is imperative that you understand there is no absolute method of calculating type other than by the possible use of a computer.

Because all characters are not the same dimensions; m is wider than d, l is narrower than G, etc., the character count charts in the type book represent an *average*. Consequently, different copy, with the same character count may fill the same area differently when converted to type. In Fig. 12 each line has the same character count and same point size.

Fig. 12

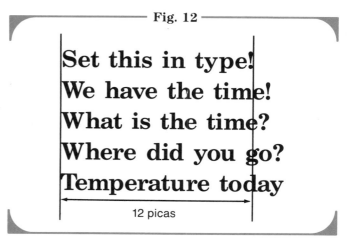

Set this in type!
We have the time!
What is the time?
Where did you go?
Temperature today

12 picas

This method of calculation is used only as a guide to approximate a setting. The more thoroughly you apply your knowledge of type and its peculiarities the closer you will get to solving your problems. The only way of knowing if a particular specification is correct is to have it set. The truth is in the setting. But you can't just go along randomly setting type until you get what you want. Unless of course you have the luxury of an unlimited budget and plenty of time.

Type calculating might be compared to a crystal ball. It is a preview of what it MIGHT look like once it has been set. By applying these principles you will be able to anticipate layout problems. You will know *before* setting the copy that it will or will not fit. You will know *before* setting the copy if it will work with your design. You will know *before* setting the copy if it needs to be cut or increased.

One disadvantage with this kind of character table is that it is calibrated for lower case averages. If you wanted to estimate the copy in all caps rather than cap and lower case you would have to guess by using a ratio of approximately—30% for caps. Here is how it could be done:

THE 30% FORMULA

First note that the exclamation point is not the size of a character. Punctuation can be considered a half cap and the same is true of the letter "i". Your character count for this setting in all caps would be 15.5 characters.

Consult the chart for 18 point.

1.35×12 picas = 16.20 characters.

$16.20 - 30\% = 11.34$ caps.

18 point will be too large.

Try 14 point.

1.74×12 picas = 20.88 characters.

$20.88 - 30\% \times 14.62$ characters.

You are working with 15.5 characters but it is close enough to conclude that 14 point will fit. Remember, this 30% formula is an approximation. You need to start somewhere and it is obvious that 12 point would be too small. But for the sake of demonstration let's set it in both 14 and 12 point. Fig. 13 is our mark up. Note that the mark up varies depending on how the original copy has been typed. Fig. 14 is the result.

The setting is very close, but notice the wide word spacing. This could easily be adjusted by closing up space between words to fit 12 picas.

End Result

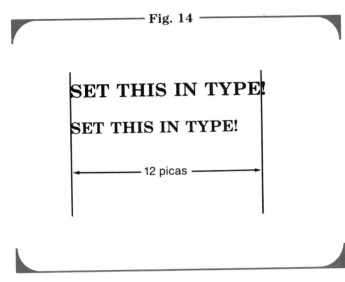

Fig. 14

SET THIS IN TYPE!

SET THIS IN TYPE!

← 12 picas →

The purpose of this chapter was to define the formula and demonstrate its application. It was also established that there are certain shortcomings in the process which must be dealt with. For example, the end result in Fig. 9 is exactly how we calculated it and it does fit the area, but it is *shorter* than 6 picas. We were only concerned with it not falling *deeper* than 6 picas. What if it *had* to be 6 picas deep? Figs. 12 and 14 present still another peculiarity of type setting that must be confronted. The remainder of this text is devoted to solving these problems and others.

This, now, is what type specification is all about.

Fig. 13

SET THIS IN TYPE! — 14 PT. Century Textbook Bold, caps

Set this in type! — 12 pt. Century Textbook Bold, caps

Chapter Three
Problems and Solutions

LINE SPACING (LEADING)

Line spacing is used to increase the overall depth of copy or to control color. Whatever the reason the procedure is the same. The space between lines is usually measured in points and half points. For example if you wanted to "open" a block of copy the amount of added space between each line would be dependent upon the depth requirements.

The Problem

The setting in Fig. 15 is 8 lines of 8/8 measuring 5.25 picas on the depth.* We want to open it to a 6 pica depth. How much line spacing is needed?

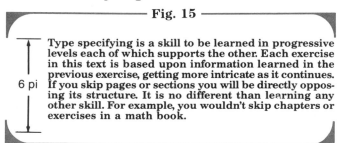

— Fig. 15 —

6 pi

Type specifying is a skill to be learned in progressive levels each of which supports the other. Each exercise in this text is based upon information learned in the previous exercise, getting more intricate as it continues. If you skip pages or sections you will be directly opposing its structure. It is no different than learning any other skill. For example, you wouldn't skip chapters or exercises in a math book.

* For simplification, when measuring lines of text it is easier to measure from the top of the ascender in the first line to the base of the last line, rather than to the last descender.

Calculation

Place your type gauge on the layout adjusting it until you find the slot where "8" most closely aligns with the 6 pica depth; Fig. 16.

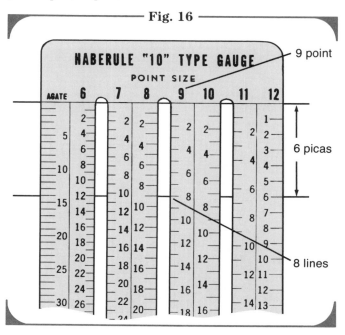

— Fig. 16 —

HABERULE "10" TYPE GAUGE

POINT SIZE

9 point

6 picas

8 lines

Observe that it is the 9 point slot in which the 8 lines will fit. If you subtract the type size (8 points) from the 9 points you will have the added line spacing of 1 point. So your spec is 8 point type on a 9 point line or 8/9.

Specification

8/9 Century Textbook Bold, × 18 picas, flush left and right, caps and lower case.

End Result

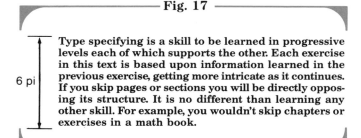

Fig. 17

6 pi

Type specifying is a skill to be learned in progressive levels each of which supports the other. Each exercise in this text is based upon information learned in the previous exercise, getting more intricate as it continues. If you skip pages or sections you will be directly opposing its structure. It is no different than learning any other skill. For example, you wouldn't skip chapters or exercises in a math book.

Do not be confused by this use of the gauge. In chapter two it was used to determine the *point size* of the type. In this calculation the same gauge was used for a different purpose. You determined how much *line spacing* you needed to fill the depth. As another example, if you wanted to open the setting to a depth of 6.5 picas you would adjust the gauge until the 8 in any slot aligned with a 6.5 pica depth; Fig. 18.

Fig. 18

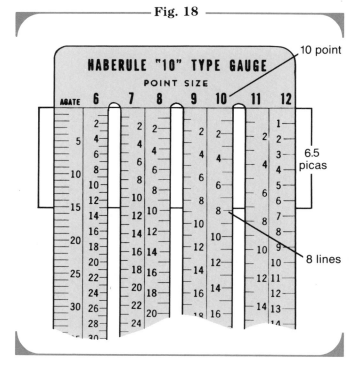

HABERULE "10" TYPE GAUGE

POINT SIZE

10 point

6.5 picas

8 lines

Note that it is the 10 point slot in which the 8 lines will fit. You would set it 8/10 to fill 6.5 picas.

The gauge, then, has two functions. One to determine the type *size*. The other to determine *line spacing*.

PRECISE DEPTH CALCULATION

The formula, as previously described for character counting text is fine for general overall speccing. However, for a more precise calculation it is advisable to character count *each paragraph*, rather than the overall copy. For example, the total *overall* count for the copy in Fig. 19 is 1059 characters. Using the chart in Fig. 20 we conclude that the copy will set to a depth of 12 lines if set in 9 point Futura Light × 30 picas; Fig. 20A.

However, the individual paragraph computation concluded a depth of 13 lines; Fig. 20 B. This could be critical. Which is correct? Let's set it and see the result.

───── **Fig. 19** ─────

Suddenly the wind acclerated. Massive sheets of piercing
rain raced across the surf at a forty-five degree angle. Bill
faltered, sinking below the surface, but somehow managed to gain
a footing and grappled his way to shore.   The wind blew with   *365*
such force he was barely able to get to his feet. Leaning hard
into the wind he looked out across the turbulent bay.

At first he thought he saw huge billowing black clouds hovering low over the bay. Through the nerve-racking, screeching
wind a low rumble could be heard and he imagined he felt the
beach tremble. The black clouds were getting closer -- fast!   *565*
Now he was certain he heard a rumble -- loud -- louder --
getting closer. The ground was definitely shaking. He spun
and ran toward the house straining against the weight of his
wet clothes and waterfilled boots. He stopped for a moment,
heaving to catch his breath in the ferocious wind and looked
back at the bay.   *129*

"My God." he screamed in disbelief. Not two hundred yards
from shore an ominous, 2-story tidal wave rumbled savagely   *1059*
toward him.

───── **Fig. 20** ─────

TYPEFACE NAME   ## CHARACTER PER PICA

	6	7	8	9	10	11	12	14	18	24	30	36	48	60	72
Futura Bold Cond. Italic Reverse (NEU) D	–	–	–	–	–	–	–	–	1.76	1.32	1.06	.88	.66	.53	.44
Futura Light (NEU) T/D	4.45	3.81	3.35	2.97	2.67	2.43	2.22	1.91	1.48	1.11	.89	.74	.56	.44	.37
Futura Light Italic II (NEU) T/D	4.60	3.94	3.45	3.07	2.76	2.51	2.30	1.97	1.53	1.15	.92	.77	.58	.46	.38
Futura Book II (NEU) T/D	4.38	3.76	3.29	2.92	2.63	2.39	2.19	1.88	1.46	1.10	.88	.73	.55	.44	.37
Futura Book Italic II (NEU) T/D	4.45	3.81	3.35	2.97	2.67	2.43	2.22	1.91	1.48	1.11	.89	.74	.56	.44	.37
Futura Medium II (NEU) T/D	4.28	3.67	3.21	2.85	2.57	2.33	2.14	1.83	1.43	1.07	.86	.71	.53	.43	.36
ura Medium Italic II (NEU) T/D	4.33	3.71		2.89	2.60	2.36	2.16	1.85	1.44	1.08	.87	.72	.54	.43	.36

2.97 × 30 pi = 89.10 per line

Overall count:

1059 ÷ 89.10 = 11.89 (12 lines)

A

Per Paragraph Count:

365 ÷ 89.10 = 4.10 (4 lines)
565 ÷ 89.10 = 6.34 (7 lines)
129 ÷ 89.10 = 1.45 (2 lines)

B   *13 lines*

Specification

The marked up copy in Fig. 21A indicates 9 point type with 1 point line spacing (9/10), justified on 30 picas.

─────────────────── **Fig. 21A** ───────────────────

2M Suddenly the wind acclerated. Massive sheets of piercing rain raced across the surf at a forty-five degree angle. Bill faltered, sinking below the surface, but somehow managed to gain a footing and grappled his way to shore. The wind blew with such force he was barely able to get to his feet. Leaning hard into the wind he looked out across the turbulent bay.

2M At first he thought he saw huge billowing black clouds hovering low over the bay. Through the nerve-racking, screeching wind a low rumble could be heard and he imagined he felt the beach tremble. The black clouds were getting closer -- fast! Now he was certain he heard a rumble -- loud -- louder -- getting closer. The ground was definitely shaking. He spun and ran toward the house straining against the weight of his wet clothes and waterfilled boots. He stopped for a moment, heaving to catch his breath in the ferocious wind and looked back at the bay.

2M "My God." he screamed in disbelief. Not two hundred yards from shore an ominous, 2-story tidal wave rumbled savagely toward him.

9/10 Futura Light II Fl L/R × 30 pi c/lc

End Result

─────────────────── **Fig. 21B** ───────────────────

Suddenly the wind accelerated. Massive sheets of piercing rain raced across the surf at a forty-five degree angle. Bill faltered, sinking below the surface, but somehow managed to gain a footing and grappled his way to shore. The wind blew with such force he was barely able to get to his feet. Leaning hard into the wind he looked out across the turbulent bay.

At first he thought he saw huge billowing black clouds hovering low over the bay. Through the nerve-racking, screeching wind a low rumble could be heard and he imagined he felt the beach tremble. The black clouds were getting closer—fast! Now he was certain he heard a rumble—loud—louder—getting closer. The ground was definitely shaking. He spun and ran toward the house straining against the weight of his wet clothes and water-filled boots. He stopped for a moment heaving to catch his breath in the ferocious wind and looked back at the bay.

"My God!" he screamed in disbelief. Not two hundred yards from shore an ominous, 2-story tidal wave rumbled savagely toward him.

13 lines
(10.5 picas)

It set 13 lines deep as anticipated in the paragraph calculation.

Paragraph counting is of course, time consuming and would be totally impractical with a lengthy manuscript. But it should be considered when speccing small amounts of copy where accuracy of depth is critical.

Color

Now let's experiment with line spacing a little. As previously mentioned, line spacing controls the depth but also affects the color. By adding 2 points line spacing to the setting in Fig. 22, making it 9/12 (or a total of 3 points of space) we increased the depth from 10.5 picas to 12.5 picas. But we also created a lighter overall color to the text.

Line spacing must be used with discretion. Three point line spacing is not esthetically the most desirable, but is passable. It depends wholly upon the type size and its function. But there is a stage where too much spacing could be considered poor design. The text in Fig. 23 was set 9/15.5. Take notice of the decided lightness in color as well as the general openness of the text. It is beginning to fall apart.

—— **Fig. 22** ——

Suddenly the wind accelerated. Massive sheets of piercing rain raced across the surf at a forty-five degree angle. Bill faltered, sinking below the surface, but somehow managed to gain a footing and grappled his way to shore. The wind blew with such force he was barely able to get to his feet. Leaning hard into the wind he looked out across the turbulent bay.

At first he thought he saw huge billowing black clouds hovering low over the bay. Through the nerve-racking, screeching wind a low rumble could be heard and he imagined he felt the beach tremble. The black clouds were getting closer—fast! Now he was certain he heard a rumble—loud—louder—getting closer. The ground was definitely shaking. He spun and ran toward the house straining against the weight of his wet clothes and water-filled boots. He stopped for a moment heaving to catch his breath in the ferocious wind and looked back at the bay.

"My God!" he screamed in disbelief. Not two hundred yards from shore an ominous, 2-story tidal wave rumbled savagely toward him.

12.5 picas

End Result

—— **Fig. 23** ——

Suddenly the wind accelerated. Massive sheets of piercing rain raced across the surf at a forty-five degree angle. Bill faltered, sinking below the surface, but somehow managed to gain a footing and grappled his way to shore. The wind blew with such force he was barely able to get to his feet. Leaning hard into the wind he looked out across the turbulent bay.

At first he thought he saw huge billowing black clouds hovering low over the bay. Through the nerve-racking, screeching wind a low rumble could be heard and he imagined he felt the beach tremble. The black clouds were getting closer—fast! Now he was certain he heard a rumble—loud—louder—getting closer. The ground was definitely shaking. He spun and ran toward the house straining against the weight of his wet clothes and water-filled boots. He stopped for a moment heaving to catch his breath in the ferocious wind and looked back at the bay.

"My God!" he screamed in disbelief. Not two hundred yards from shore an ominous, 2-story tidal wave rumbled savagely toward him.

If you are not restricted to the 9 point size you could recalculate it in a *larger* size to the *same depth*. The setting in Fig. 24 is 11/13. There is a noticeable difference in color as well as readability. There is more to it than meets the eye.

Here is the formula for quick calculation to determine the additional line spacing needed to increase the depth but not the type size.

- Measure the additional space in points.
- Count the spaces between lines.
- Divide it into the total points to be added and you

have the additional line spacing needed to fill the depth.

For example, the additional space may be 3.5 picas, which is a total of 42 points.

- The total number of spaces between lines is 14.
- Divide 14 into 42 to get 3 points.

This means if you added 3 points to the line spacing the copy will set 3.5 picas deeper. Figure 24 is set 11/13 to a depth of 16 picas. If you added 3 points to the line spacing, making it 11/16, the total depth would be 19.5 picas.

--- **Fig. 24** ---

Suddenly the wind accelerated. Massive sheets of piercing rain raced across the surf at a forty-five degree angle. Bill faltered, sinking below the surface, but somehow managed to gain a footing and grappled his way to shore. The wind blew with such force he was barely able to get to his feet. Leaning hard into the wind he looked out across the turbulent bay.

At first he thought he saw huge billowing black clouds hovering low over the bay. Through the nerve-racking, screeching wind a low rumble could be heard and he imagined he felt the beach tremble. The black clouds were getting closer—fast! Now he was certain he heard a rumble—loud—louder—getting closer. The ground was definitely shaking. He spun and ran toward the house straining against the weight of his wet clothes and water-filled boots. He stopped for a moment heaving to catch his breath in the ferocious wind and looked back at the bay.

"My God!" he screamed in disbelief. Not two hundred yards from shore an ominous, 2-story tidal wave rumbled savagely toward him.

Chapter Four
Format Variations

Until now we have dealt with the basics of type specification. You have been introduced to the formula, how to read a type style character chart and how to mark up a simple block of copy. You should have an understanding of line spacing, its computation and application, as well as an introduction to terminology and symbols. By now, you should appreciate the diversity of the type gauge.

It is really quite simple in principle. What you need now is to learn to combine it all with the use of symbols to achieve much more than speccing a simple block of copy. In order to sum up what you have learned at this point, Fig. 25 illustrates the five basic text formats most commonly used. It shows the mark up as it would appear on the manuscript along with the final setting. Study them carefully. If you understand them you will realize that you have progressed through the first phase of becoming a professional type specifier. Most everyone can do this. You are now ready for the next phase.

YOU AND YOUR TYPOGRAPHER

Here are some rules.

Always keep in mind that you are the closest one to the job. You understand it because you are directly involved in it, but the typesetter will be seeing it for the first time. Do not take for granted that he will understand what it is you want him to do, no matter how simple it may seem. Your instructions must be clearly stated using the proper marks, symbols and terminology. *Do not invent your own terminology*. You must speak to him in his own language if you intend to communicate. His role is to follow your instructions. Do not depend on his "interpreting" what you want. If your specifications are wrong the chances are they will be set wrong. This is not to say that your typesetter is oblivious to your needs. He does want to give you the best service he can and will "get into" the job and often question what doesn't seem right to him. A good, reliable, attentive typographer is most valuable.

Handwriting your specifications is of course, unavoidable. We all feel that everyone can read our handwriting, but this may not be so. If your writing looks like a doctor's prescription, you're in for trouble. Be absolutely sure that your specifications are legible and in organized groups rather than scattered all over the page.

Until you have had enough experience to feel confident that your mark up is understandable it may be helpful to show it to a fellow worker. If he doesn't understand it and you find yourself explaining it to him, it may be best to redo it.

Another very helpful approach that I strongly recommend is to call your typographer, alert him that you're

Fig. 25

$\frac{9}{10}$ TS *Martin Gothic Light*

fl. L/R x 14 pi

no hyphens

Type specifying is a skill to be learned in progressive levels each of which supports the other. Each exercise in this text is based upon information learned in the previous exercise, getting more intricate as it continues. If you skip pages or sections you will be directly opposing its structure. It is no different than learning any other skill. You wouldn't skip chapters or exercises in a math book.

$\frac{9}{10}$ TS *Martin Gothic Light*

fl. left, rag right x max. 14 pi

Type specifying is a skill to be learned in progressive levels each of which supports the other. Each exercise in this text is based upon information learned in the previous exercise, getting more intricate as it continues. If you skip pages or sections you will be directly opposing its structure. It is no different than learning any other skill. You wouldn't skip chapters or exercises in a math book.

$\frac{9}{10}$ TS *Martin Gothic Light, rag left, fl. right x 14 pi*

Type specifying is a skill to be learned in progressive levels each of which supports the other. Each exercise in this text is based upon information learned in the previous exercise, getting more intricate as it continues. If you skip pages or sections you will be directly opposing its structure. It is no different than learning any other skill. You wouldn't skip chapters or exercises in a math book.

$\frac{9}{10}$ TS *Martin Gothic Light*

Rag R & L x max. 14 pi

Type specifying is a skill to be learned in progressive levels each of which supports the other. Each exercise in this text is based upon information learned in the previous exercise, getting more intricate as it continues. If you skip pages or sections you will be directly opposing its structure. It is no different than learning any other skill. You wouldn't skip chapters or exercises in a math book.

$\frac{9}{10}$ TS *Martin Gothic Light, centered lines x max. 14 pi Break each line as indicated on manuscript*

Type specifying is a skill to be learned in progressive levels each of which supports the other. Each exercise in this text is based upon information learned in the previous exercise, getting more intricate as it continues. If you skip pages or sections you will be directly opposing its structure. It is no different than learning any other skill. You wouldn't skip chapters or exercises in a math book.

sending a job and if he has any questions to please call you. It wouldn't hurt to tell him you are new at type speccing or that you're not certain he will understand your mark up. It is likely he will be cooperative and contribute to developing your skill. It is all a matter of communication between you and your typesetter. Become his friend.

THE TYPE TISSUE

A type tissue is an accurate layout drawing (usually done on tracing paper) of the format to be followed in setting type. It is often sent to the typographer along with the marked up copy to help him visualize what he must do.

The tissue can also carry some of the specs making the copy mark up easier to understand. For example, Fig. 26A shows the marked up copy and the character chart 26B used to calculate the specs. Note the circled numbers to the right of the copy. They are the character counts for each paragraph. These would not appear on your copy when you send it to the typesetter. They are shown here to help you understand the example. Study it carefully by reading the specs, referring to the chart, counting the characters and calculating. By now you should understand these specs. Note the indication for 2 pica paragraph indents, paragraph spacing and bold face. Did you catch the subtle line break indication in the two last paragraphs?

—— **Fig. 26A** ——

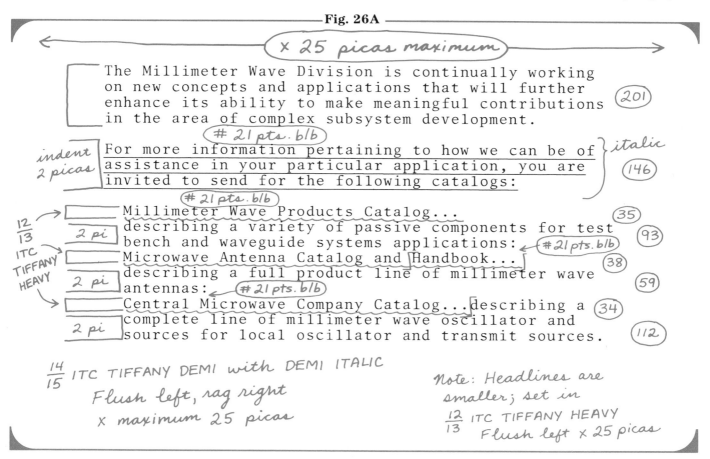

—— **Fig. 26B** ——

TYPEFACE NAME	CHARACTER PER PICA														
	6	7	8	9	10	11	12	14	18	24	30	36	48	60	72
Tiffany Light (ITC) T	4.36	3.74	3.27	2.91	2.62	2.38	2.18	1.87	1.45	1.09	—	—	—	—	—
Tiffany Light (ITC) D	—	—	—	—	—	—	—	1.71	1.33	1.00	.80	.66	.50	.40	.33
Tiffany Medium (ITC) T	4.02	3.45	3.02	2.68	2.41	2.19	2.01	1.72	1.33	1.00	—	—	—	—	—
Tiffany Medium (ITC) D	—	—	—	—	—	—	—	1.59	1.24	.93	.74	.62	.46	.37	.31
Tiffany Demi (ITC) T	4.02	3.45	3.02	2.68	2.41	2.19	2.01	1.72	1.33	1.00	—	—	—	—	—
Tiffany Demi (ITC) D	—	—	—	—	—	—	—	1.55	1.20	.90	.72	.60	.45	.36	.30
Tiffany Heavy (ITC) T	3.41	2.92	2.56	2.27	2.05	1.86	1.70	1.46	1.13	.85	—	—	—	—	—
Tiffany Heavy (ITC) D	—	—	—	—	—	—	—	1.35	1.05	.79	.63	.52	.39	.31	.26
Tiffany Light Italic (ITC) T/D	4.20	3.60	3.15	2.80	2.52	2.29	2.10	1.80	1.40	1.05	.84	.70	.52	.42	.35
Tiffany Medium Italic (ITC) T/D	4.20	3.60	3.15	2.80	2.52	2.29	2.10	1.80	1.40	1.05	.84	.70	.52	.42	.35
Tiffany Demi Italic (ITC) T/D	4.10	3.52	3.08	2.74	2.46	2.24	2.05	1.76	1.37	1.03	.82	.68	.51	.41	.34
Tiffany Heavy Italic (ITC) T/D	3.42	2.93	2.57	2.28	2.05	1.87	1.71	1.47	1.14	.86	.68	.57	.43	.34	.29

———— Fig. 27 ————

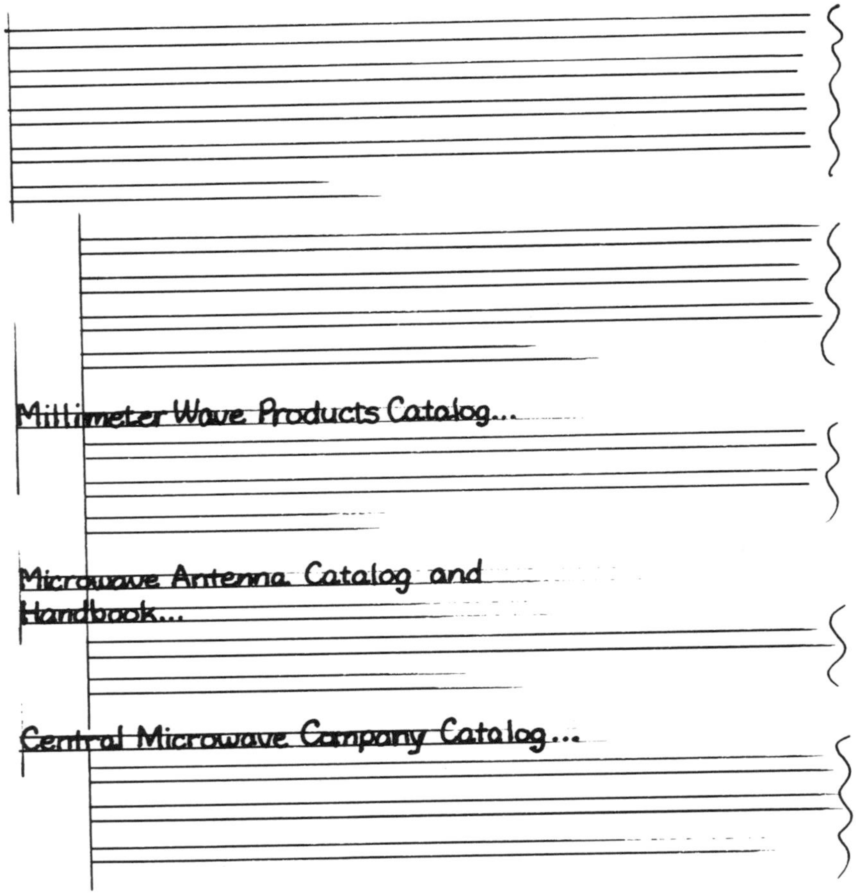

Millimeter Wave Products Catalog...

Microwave Antenna Catalog and
Handbook...

Central Microwave Company Catalog...

Type tissue

—— Fig. 28 ——

The Millimeter Wave Division is continually working on new concepts and applications that will further enhance its ability to make meaningful contributions in the area of complex subsystem development.

For more information pertaining to how we can be of assistance in your particular application, you are invited to send for the following catalogs:

Millimeter Wave Products Catalog...
describing a variety of passive components for test bench and waveguide systems applications;

Microwave Antenna Catalog and Handbook...
describing a full product line of millimeter wave antennas;

Central Microwave Company Catalog...
describing a complete line of millimeter wave oscillators and sources for local oscillator and transmit sources.

End result

HOW TO PREPARE A TISSUE

Preparing a tissue layout is simple enough once you have decided on the type size, line spacing and character count. For example, the circled numbers to the right of the manuscript in Fig. 26 are the character counts for each paragraph. Using the chart in Fig. 26, calculate the line count for each paragraph in 14 point type. Then, using the "15" slot on your gauge (the setting is to be 14/15), tick off the lineage for each paragraph, boxing them in according to the specified widths.

Line spacing in computer typography is programmed from the *base* of one line to the *base* of the *next* line. If you want to *add* 6 points of space between paragraphs, add 6 points to the already established 14/15 making it 14/21. Thus your markup would be an indication for 21 points of space from the "base" of one line to the "base" of the following line. Notice the indication "#21 pts b/b" for additional paragraph spacing; Fig. 26A.

Another method of indicating additional space is "+1 line" or "+ ½ line," etc. If your spec is 14/15, "+ 1 line means plus 15 points, making your new spec 14/30; "+ ½ line" means plus 7.5 points (14/22.5). The "line" is the *bottom* number in your spec; Fig. 29.

--- **Fig. 29** ---

30 pts. b/b >

The Millimeter Wave Division is continually working on new concepts and applications that will further enhance its ability to make meaningful contributions in the area of complex subsystem development.

For more information pertaining to how we can be of assistance in your particular application, you are invited to send for the following catalogs:

The Millimeter Wave Division is continually working on new concepts and applications that will further enhance its ability to make meaningful contributions in the area of complex subsystem development.

+1 li >

For more information pertaining to how we can be of assistance in your particular application, you are invited to send for the following catalogs:

Both of the above indications have the same meaning

The Millimeter Wave Division is continually working on new concepts and applications that will further enhance its ability to make meaningful contributions in the area of complex subsystem development.

22.5 pts. > b/b

For more information pertaining to how we can be of assistance in your particular application, you are invited to send for the following catalogs:

The Millimeter Wave Division is continually working on new concepts and applications that will further enhance its ability to make meaningful contributions in the area of complex subsystem development.

+ ½ li >

For more information pertaining to how we can be of assistance in your particular application, you are invited to send for the following catalogs:

Both of the above indications have the same meaning

RUN-AROUND SETTING

Fig. 30

The established layout in Fig. 30 indicates a portion of the text to be set narrower in order to accommodate a photo, a large capital letter, a design element or whatever you choose.

The layout, type face, size and leading have already been established. Therefore, before marking up the copy for this kind of layout it is advisable to spec it to be certain it will fit properly.

- Measure the layout. The narrower portion is 13 picas while the wider section measures 22 picas.
- Consult your type chart to find the character count for each of these line widths.
   The established type face and size is:
   9/10 pt. Helvetica
   13 picas = 37 characters
   22 picas = 62 characters
- Character count each paragraph of the copy and indicate your totals in the margin; Fig. 31.

Fig. 31

Since 1972, Tomac Industries has been a leading supplier of high quality components and subsystems for the microwave industry. These products cover an entire spectrum of applications involving the generation, amplification, detection and control of microwave energy. They are installed in a variety of commercial systems, in conjunction with radar, guidance electronics and communications hardware.

$$\begin{array}{r} 384 \\ 15 \\ \hline 399 \end{array}$$

Down through the years, Tomac has enjoyed an enviable reputation for developing a complete line of quality products that have become known for their consistent emphasis on reliability, performance and cost effectiveness. Through a consistent policy of selective growth, the company has reached a point where it can demonstrate a unique capacity for designing, building and integrating the most complete line of components and subsystems in the industry.

$$\begin{array}{r} 368 \\ 44 \\ 42 \\ \hline 454 \end{array}$$

The latest expression of this capability involves a new line of ultra-sophisticated millimeter wave supercomponents that integrate many complex functions into one miniaturized package. Starting with the design and development of millimeter wave antennas, this effort has expanded to include a complete line of mixers, converters and detectors, which are described in this brochure.

$$\begin{array}{r} 329 \\ 36 \\ 17 \\ \hline 382 \end{array}$$

- Now count the number of lines of the 13 pica width indicated on the layout (9 lines). Multiply 9 lines by 37 characters (333).
- Subtract 333 from the total number of characters in the first paragraph. This leaves 66 characters to start the first line of the 22 pica measure. If 62 characters will fill one line x 22 pi, it is doubtful that 66 characters would go to a second line. Ignore the 4 extra characters.
- Divide 62 into the character count for the second paragraph to find the number of lines it will occupy.

$$62 \overline{)\,454}^{\;7.32}$$

Rounded to 8 lines

- Repeat this with the last paragraph

$$62 \overline{)\,382}^{\;6.16}$$

Rounded to 7 lines

- Add the total number of lines for each paragraph (25) and compare it with the layout; Fig. 32.

--- **Fig. 32** ---

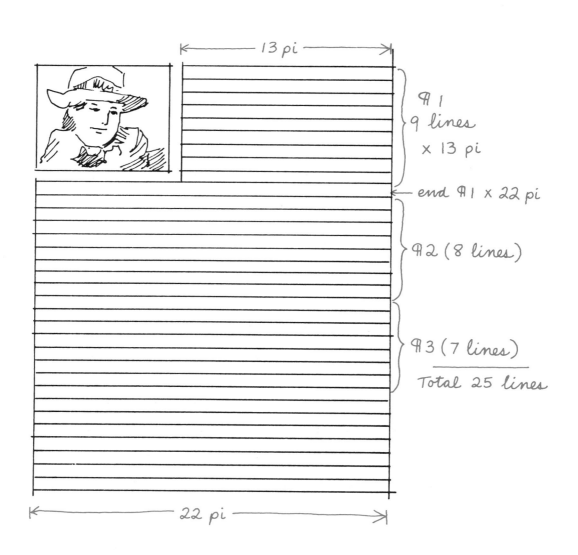

––––––––––––––– Fig. 33A –––––––––––––––

$\frac{9}{10}$ *HELVETICA, FLUSH LEFT & RIGHT*
  SET AS PER ATTACHED LAYOUT

Since 1972, Tomac Industries has been a leading
supplier of high quality components and subsystems
for the microwave industry. These products cover
an entire spectrum of applications involving the
generation, amplification, detection and control
of microwave energy. They are installed in a variety
of commercial systems, in conjunction with radar,
guidance electronics and communications hardware.

NO EXTRA LINE-SPACE BETWEEN PARAGRAPHS

Down through the years, Tomac has enjoyed an enviable
reputation for developing a complete line of quality
products that have become known for their consistent
emphasis on reliability, performance and cost
effectiveness. Through a consistent policy of
selective growth, the company has reached a point where
it can demonstrate a unique capacity for designing,
building and integrating the most complete line of
components and subsystems in the industry.

The latest expression of this capability involves a
new line of ultra-sophisticated millimeter wave
supercomponents that integrate many complex functions
into one miniaturized package. Starting with the
design and development of millimeter wave antennas,
this effort has expanded to include a complete line of
mixers, converters and detectors, which are described
in this brochure.

Fig. 33B

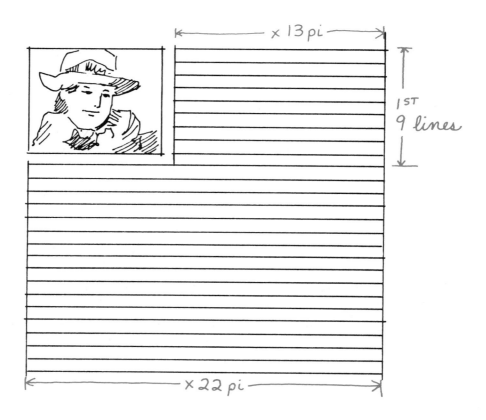

According to your calculation, using 9/10, the copy will actually fall 8 lines shorter than the layout indicates. The question at this time is how closely you must adhere to the layout. If the depth is arbitrary leave the spec as it is. If not, you will have to decide on an alternative solution, i.e.: open or close the copy with line spacing, make the type larger or smaller, consider revising the layout, etc.

It might be helpful if you prepared a revised layout indicating your estimated number of lines to avoid confusion. Your mark up and tissue would be as shown in Fig. 33A/B.

CONTOURED SETTING

Fig. 34

The layout in Fig. 34 requires the type to be set around the shape of the art.

The easiest approach would be to make a very accurate tissue of the layout shape. Send it along with the copy to the typesetter with an indication of the type face, size and leading, and the instructions "set to fit as per layout." Then hope for the best; Fig. 35.

This is too expensive a setting to simply *hope* that the type size and lead is correct for this amount of copy. It could result in a bad setting or a call from the typesetter telling you there is too much copy or too little to fit in 9 point – what should he do? Close up the space? Change the size? Open the space? Change the width?

Once again, if cost or time is not a factor, then you can continue experimenting with the setting until you are satisfied with the results.

Remember the typesetter is not the art director. He is simply trying to give you what *you* want. You must be specific.

It is advisable that you anticipate problems before ordering the type. This does not mean you should expend endless energy trying to spec with mechanical precision. It can't be done in the first place. But you can at least get as close as possible to what you want in the first setting.

It often takes two attempts to accomplish a good contour setting. The first one generally presents unforeseen, physical limitations such as copy being too short, too many hyphenations or irregular word spacing. For this reason it is best to order "reader's proofs" before going into reproduction proofs.

Start by establishing a preferred type face, size and leading. Let's see how 9/10 Helios Light would fit.

In order to calculate the character fit for this kind of layout you must measure and character count *each line* because they are different lengths. However, you might try a short cut by using an average line length which would be 23 picas.

Using the 10 slot on your scale, measure the overall depth of the layout in Fig. 34 to determine the number of lines it will occupy (26 lines).

The chart indicates 2.93 characters in one pica for 9 point Helios. Multiply 2.93 by 23 to equal 67 characters for one line.

Multiply the line depth (26) by the characters per line (67) to equal 1742 characters.

The character count for the copy (Fig. 35) is 1235, leaving a difference of 507 characters.

You have concluded that 9/10 is too small. It will be

— **Fig. 35** —

no ¶ indents

$\frac{9}{10}$ *Helios Light*

*Contour left
as per attached
layout.*

Flush right.

Since 1972, Tomac Industries has been a leading supplier of high quality components and subsystems for the microwave industry. These products cover an entire spectrum of applications involving the generation, amplification, detection and control of microwave energy. They are installed in a variety of commercial systems, in conjunction with radar, guidance electronics and communications hardware.

14 pts. b/b ¶ #

Down through the years, Tomac has enjoyed an enviable reputation for developing a complete line of quality products that have become known for their consistent emphasis on reliability, performance and cost effectiveness. Through a consistent policy of selective growth, the company has reached a point where it can demonstrate a unique capacity for designing, building and integrating the most complete line of components and subsystems in the industry.

14 pts. b/b ¶ #

The latest expression of this capability involves a new line of ultra-sophisticated millimeter wave supercomponents that integrate many complex functions into one miniaturized package. Starting with the design and development of millimeter wave antennas, this effort has expanded to include a complete line of mixers, converters and detectors, which are described in this brochure.

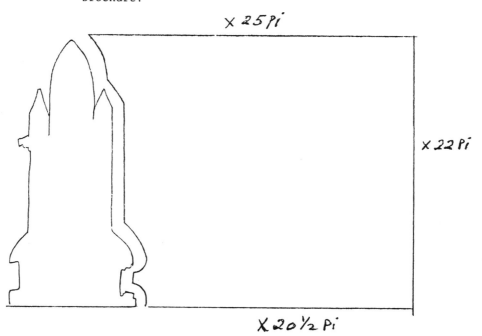

X 25 Pi

X 22 Pi

X 20½ Pi

short by 507 characters. Had you ordered it as such it would have been set wrong. An unnecessary waste. This is a perfect example of the advantage of pre-calculation.

Try another size. Let's jump to 11/12.

According to the chart, one pica equals 2.40 which would make one line 55 characters. But now you have to re-measure the depth using the 12 slot to determine the new number of lines (22).

Multiply 22 by 55 to equal 1210 which is as close as one could get. It is best to be slightly under than over the total count.

Chances are, this calculation will work. You know that 9 point is much too small and that 12 point may be too large. So you have to go with 11 point. Of course, if you do not want to use 11 point for some reason you will have to consider copy or layout revisions.

If you had the time or the inclination to work out a more accurate calculation you could spec it line-for-line. Let's run through it just to see how closely the average count compares.

Start by measuring the first line (25 picas).

$$25 \times 2.40 = 60$$

Measure the second line (24½ picas).

$$24.50 \times 2.40 = 59$$

Repeat this to the last line. Then total the line counts; Fig. 36.

— **Fig. 36** —

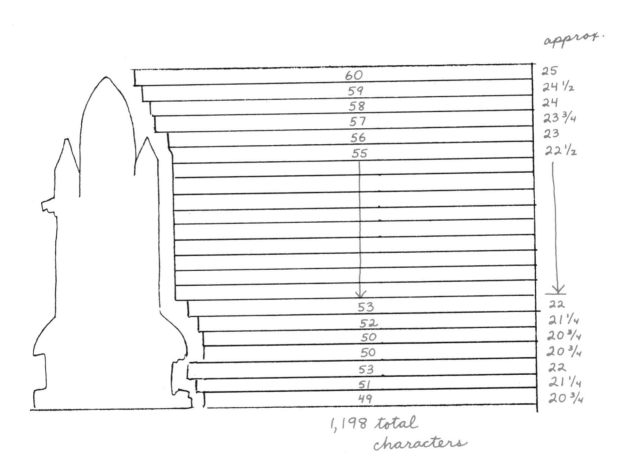

approx.

count	picas
60	25
59	24 ½
58	24
57	23 ¾
56	23
55	22 ½
53	22
52	21 ¼
50	20 ¾
50	20 ¾
53	22
51	21 ¼
49	20 ¾

1,198 *total characters*

The count for copy is 1235.
The average type count is 1210.
The line-for-line type count is 1198.

You may as well use the "average" formula. It's less time consuming and appears to be adequate. It is your decision.

When the type setter receives a layout such as this, each line must be measured in order to program the equipment. It would be a big help if you at least indicated the pica lengths of each line on your layout. The line-for-line character count is not necessary.

To sum it up, we have decided that 11/12 Helios Light will work, but as a matter of caution we will order "reader's proofs" for checking. Fig. 37 is the first setting, which is incredibly close. Even the last line ran the full measure.

However, you may want to refine it further. You may not care for the three-in-a-row hyphenated lines. But you are certainly off to a good start. You can now discuss it, mark it up for revisions, leave it as is or whatever is necessary. Then order reproduction proofs.

Fig. 37

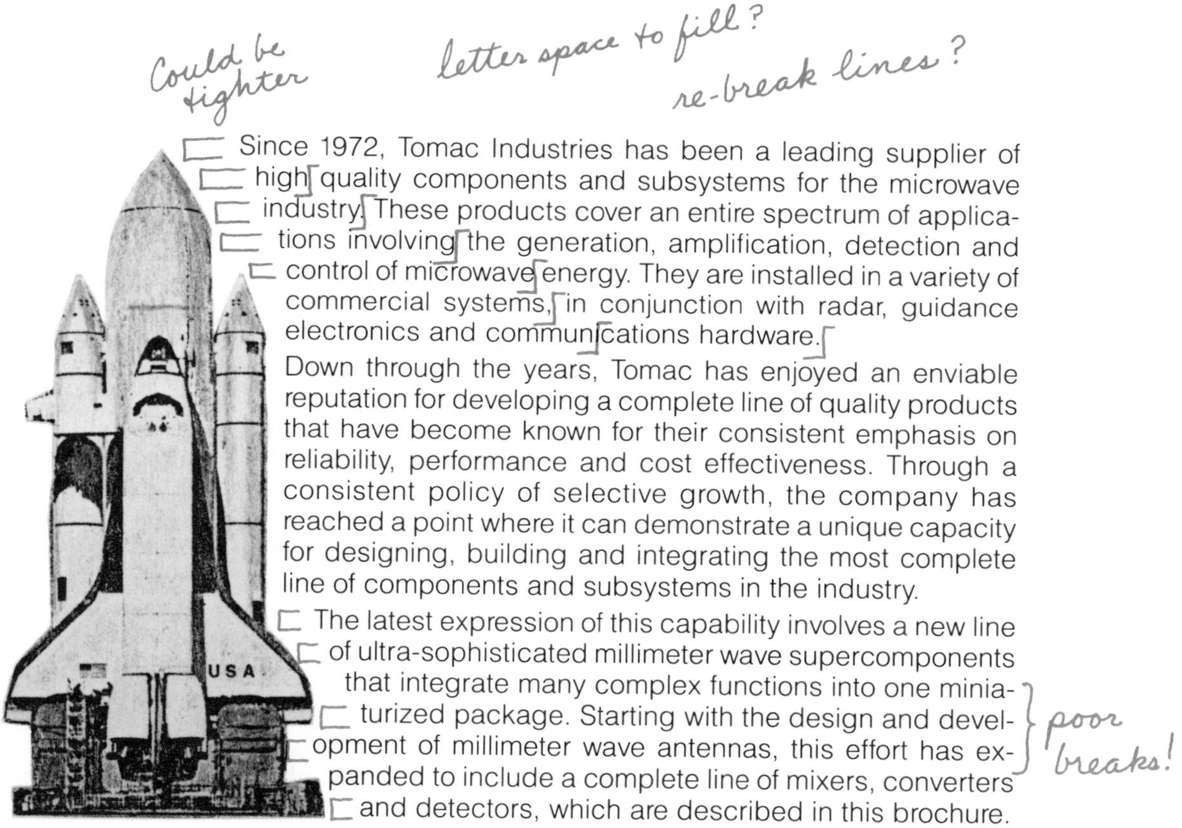

Could be tighter

letter space to fill?

re-break lines?

Since 1972, Tomac Industries has been a leading supplier of high quality components and subsystems for the microwave industry. These products cover an entire spectrum of applications involving the generation, amplification, detection and control of microwave energy. They are installed in a variety of commercial systems, in conjunction with radar, guidance electronics and communications hardware.

Down through the years, Tomac has enjoyed an enviable reputation for developing a complete line of quality products that have become known for their consistent emphasis on reliability, performance and cost effectiveness. Through a consistent policy of selective growth, the company has reached a point where it can demonstrate a unique capacity for designing, building and integrating the most complete line of components and subsystems in the industry.

The latest expression of this capability involves a new line of ultra-sophisticated millimeter wave supercomponents that integrate many complex functions into one miniaturized package. Starting with the design and development of millimeter wave antennas, this effort has expanded to include a complete line of mixers, converters and detectors, which are described in this brochure.

poor breaks!

SUBHEADS

A subhead is a subordinate headline.

The copy in Fig. 38 indicates three bold subheads, all caps, to be set in a different face and size than the text.

--- **Fig. 38** ---

MILLIMETER WAVES . . . A NEW CHAPTER

The latest expression of this capability involves a new line of ulstrasophisticated millimeter wave supercomponents that integrate many complex functions into one miniaturized package. Starting with the design and development of millimeter wave antennas, this effort has expanded to include a complete line of mixers, converters and detectors, which are described in this brochure.

COST EFFECTIVE MASS PRODUCTION TECHNIQUES

In specific terms, we have mastered production techniques that can lower design cost, while assuring that the resulting technology can be applied to standard requirements. A typical example can be found in the selection of transmission media for our mixer line where the use of fused silica suspended stripline diodes has proven superior to the use of conventional microstrip as an alternative to the same configuration.

OUR NEW MIXER AND PREAMPLIFIER DEVELOPMENT TECHNIQUES

An example involving the application of our technology to a practical requirement can be found in the development of our mixer and reamplifier. The accompanying photographs illustrate various stages in the construction and assembly of these receivers, which are shown in conjunction with an integral IF amplifier.

The specs for this exercise are as follows:

Subheads - 12/13 PT Korinna Bold, caps
Text - 10/11 Helvetica Light, caps and
lower case
Column width - 13 picas

First you must decide how the subheads are to be treated. Do you want them to be flush left and rag right? Do you want to avoid hyphenations? Should they be set as centered lines? Should they be set justified to the width of the text columns?

Very often these questions are resolved during the layout stage. The answer is dependent upon many determining factors such as esthetics, readability, the length of the subheads, the type face, the size.

For the purpose of this exercise let's set them flush left, rag right with no hyphenations.

Your main concern is how the subheads will fit in 12 point caps. Consult your type book to determine a line count for 13 picas.

Some of the more elaborate type specimen books may have character count charts for capitals, most do not. There are books with examples of capital settings in various sizes, there are those that show samples of the entire alphabet in various sizes and many simply have the alphabet in one size.

This may or may not present a problem because you have no choice but to create your own character count. As an exercise, using the example of 12 point Korinna Bold in Fig. 39, measure the number of caps in 13 picas.

— Fig. 39 —

Typography's function is to convey a visual messa
ge quickly and easily. The typographer's aim shou
ld be to aid easy legibility. He can do this by choos
ing the most readable typeface for a given proble
*Typography's function is to convey a visual me
ssage quickly and easily. The typographer's ai*
TYPOGRAPHY'S FUNCTION IS TO CONVEY A

12 PT • 13 LF • 12 S

If you were to measure 13 picas from the first character (T) to the space between FUNCTION and IS, you would get *about* 20½. Count the apostrophe as ½.

Should you measure from the beginning of the word FUNCTION you would get 21½ if you counted each I as ½. Measuring again from the beginning of the S in

TYPOGRAPHY'S you would count 21¾ counting the I as ½. The point is that you can't really get an accurate count with this kind of setting. So average it out to 21.

Another kind of type specimen example is Fig. 40 in which you see both text in caps as well as an alphabet. Count each to see if there is a difference.

— Fig. 40 —

TASTE IN PRINTING DETERMINES THE FORM TY
pography is to take. The selection of a congruous ty
peface, the quality and suitability for the purpose of
the paper to be used, the care and labor, time and co
st of materials devoted to its production, all in a dire
ct ratio to its ultimate worth and destination. Taste

ABCDEFGHIJKLMNOPQRSTUVWXYZ&
abcdefghijklmnopqrstuvwxyz
ÇÑçéíñß
1234567890
(.,:;''* ¿?¡!«»)%¢$/£

Fig. 41

A = $\frac{12}{13}$ KORINNA BOLD CAPS *flush left*

B = HELVETICA LIGHT × 13 pi *flush L/R c/lc*

(A) MILLIMETER WAVES . . . . A NEW CHAPTER   *no u/s*

(B) The latest expression of this capability involves a new line of ulstrasophisticated millimeter wave supercomponents that integrate many complex functions into one miniaturized package. Starting with the design and development of millimeter wave antennas, this effort has expanded to include a complete line of mixers, converters and detectors, which are described in this brochure.

+ 3 pts. #

(A) COST EFFECTIVE MASS PRODUCTION TECHNIQUES

(B) In specific terms, we have mastered production techniques that can lower design cost, while assuring that the resulting technology can be applied to standard requirements. A typical example can be found in the selection of transmission media for our mixer line where the use of fused silica suspended stripline diodes has proven superior to the use of conventional microstrip as an alternative to the same configuration.

+ 3 pts. #

(A) OUR NEW MIXER AND PREAMPLIFIER DEVELOPMENT TECHNIQUES

(B) An example involving the application of our technology to a practical requirement can be found in the development of our mixer and reamplifier. The accompanying photographs illustrate various stages in the construction and assembly of these receivers, which are shown in conjunction with an integral IF amplifier.

Counting from the T in TASTE (I = ½) we get 21½.

Counting from A in the alphabet we get 17½, which is a considerable difference.

Now what do we do? Which of these counts should we use? Average it out to 19.50.

Refer back to Fig. 39. Note the copy 12 PT. 13 LF. 12S below the block. This is the code for the letterspacing ratio (line feed) in the equipment used by this particular typographer. Another type shop having the same equipment may have an entirely different line feed. This would account for a variance in character count. The point is not to use the book from one type shop and order from another; you'll have problems.

What are your options? I would suggest using averages or simply go with the 30% formula if nothing else is available.

In any event you have to rely upon the count for the typographer you will use. If you set the type according to the chart in Fig. 39 the average count would be 21. In marking up the copy you will character count the headline with 21 as your maximum, taking logical breaks into consideration.

As an experiment let's set DEVELOPMENT TECHNIQUES (in the last heading) on one line, although the count is 21½.

Study the mark up in Fig. 41. Note the use of the code for simplification. Also note the deletion of underscores and change to bold face; "no u/s" means no underscore.

We took the chance and lost. The heading is too wide by one character in the last paragraph. But it is not a tragedy. All you have to do is cut it apart and put TECHNIQUES on the next line, providing you have the room to make the copy deeper.

Another solution would be to photostat this headline down to 13 picas. The others should also be statted in the same focus so that they will all be the same size.

Fig. 42

MILLIMETER WAVES... A NEW CHAPTER

The latest expression of this capability involves a new line of ultra-sophisticated millimeter wave supercomponents that integrate many complex functions into one miniaturized package. Starting with the design and development of millimeter wave antennas, this effort has expanded to include a complete line of mixers, converters and detectors, which are described in this brochure.

COST EFFECTIVE MASS PRODUCTION TECHNIQUES

In specific terms, we have mastered production techniques that can lower design cost, while assuring that the resulting technology can be applied to standard requirements. A typical example can be found in the selection of transmission media for our mixer line where the use of fused silica suspended stripline diodes has proven superior to the use of conventional microstrip as an alternative to the same configuration.

OUR NEW MIXER AND PREAMPLIFIER DEVELOPMENT TECHNIQUES

An example involving the application of our technology to a practical requirement can be found in the development of our mixer and preamplifier. The accompanying photographs illustrate various stages in the construction and assembly of these receivers, which are shown in conjunction with an integral IF amplifier.

This would be an appropriate time to spot-check your progress. Can you mark up the layout shown on this page? See how well you can do. The "T" is Craw Clarendon. The text is 12 pt. ITC Benguiat Medium.

The answer is on page 97.

Chapter Five
The Headline

PHOTO-DISPLAY TYPE

Most photographic display (headline) setting systems photograph one character at a time onto a strip of paper. Because the operator can see the letters as they are being recorded, he has the flexibility of controlling the letterspacing. The end product is a strip of type set in a continuous line to your specified height (or width) and letterspacing. The strips can then be cut apart and pasted up as you wish in a mechanical; Fig. 43.

Should time not permit you to cut and assemble the strips, or if the layout is too intricate to be pasted up, it may be best for you to have the type set in position. You will have to supply the typesetter with a well defined layout or type tissue to be used as a guide. You will then receive a proof of the headline assembled as per your type tissue or layout, ready to be placed into the mechanical; Fig. 44.

Photo headline typesetting has much to offer the designer. It can be customized to match a layout, i.e., it can be condensed, expanded, italicized, back slanted, set in an arc, a circle, overlapping letters, etc. For special settings it is advisable to prepare a layout and consult your typesetter before ordering. Discuss it with him and above all take his suggestions seriously.

HOW TO ORDER PHOTO HEADLINES

Because photo headlines are usually ordered to specific sizes to meet layout requirements it is best to use either inches or picas as a unit of measurement rather than points. A standard approach in determining size is to measure the *cap height* or the lower case "x" *height* as it is to appear in your layout; Fig. 45.

Your next step is to specify the kind of spacing you want. All photo display books should have a showing of the various letterspacing available; Fig. 46.

Now you are ready to mark up your copy. Be certain that the required copy is properly typewritten in caps and/or lower case as required. If it is to be set in position, you should also supply the typesetter with a layout to be followed with your specs indicated on the copy sheet or layout.

Unlike text settings where you are supplied with 1 or 2 duplicate proofs, photo headline settings produce only *one* original (unless you request more than one). Your markup should look like Fig. 47.

You are not restricted to ordering headline type on the character height. You can order it on the width. However, if you specify a headline to be set on the *height* you cannot be sure how *wide* it will be. Likewise, should you order

─── **Fig. 43** ───

IMPORTANT! IF YOU OWN A

COMPACT DISC PLAYER THERE

IS SOMETHING

YOU SHOULD KNOW.

Photo headline strips

IMPORTANT!
IF YOU OWN A COMPACT DISC PLAYER
THERE IS SOMETHING YOU SHOULD KNOW.

Mechanical assembly

─── **Fig. 44** ───

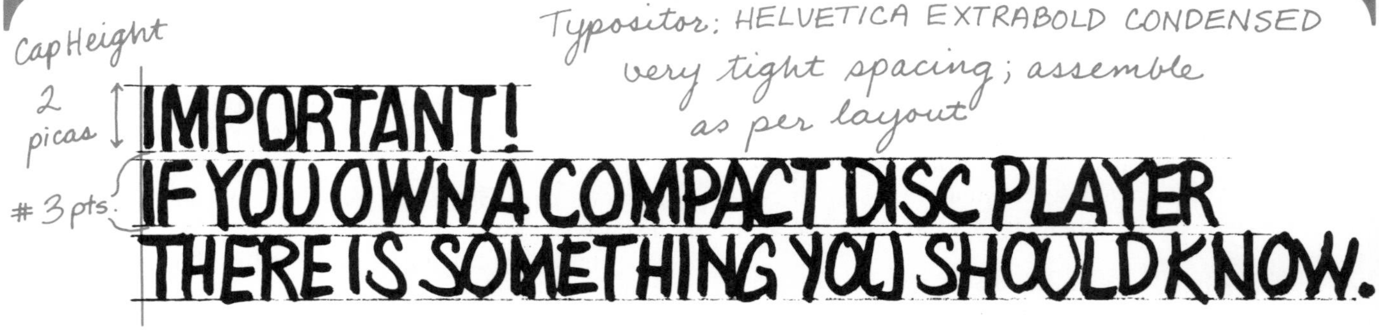

Cap Height
2 picas
picas
3 pts.

Typositor: HELVETICA EXTRABOLD CONDENSED
very tight spacing; assemble
as per layout

IMPORTANT!
IF YOU OWN A COMPACT DISC PLAYER
THERE IS SOMETHING YOU SHOULD KNOW.

Layout

─── Fig. 45 ───

Distribution System

"CAP"
Height
(in picas or inches)

"X" Height
(in picas
or inches)

─── Fig. 46 ───

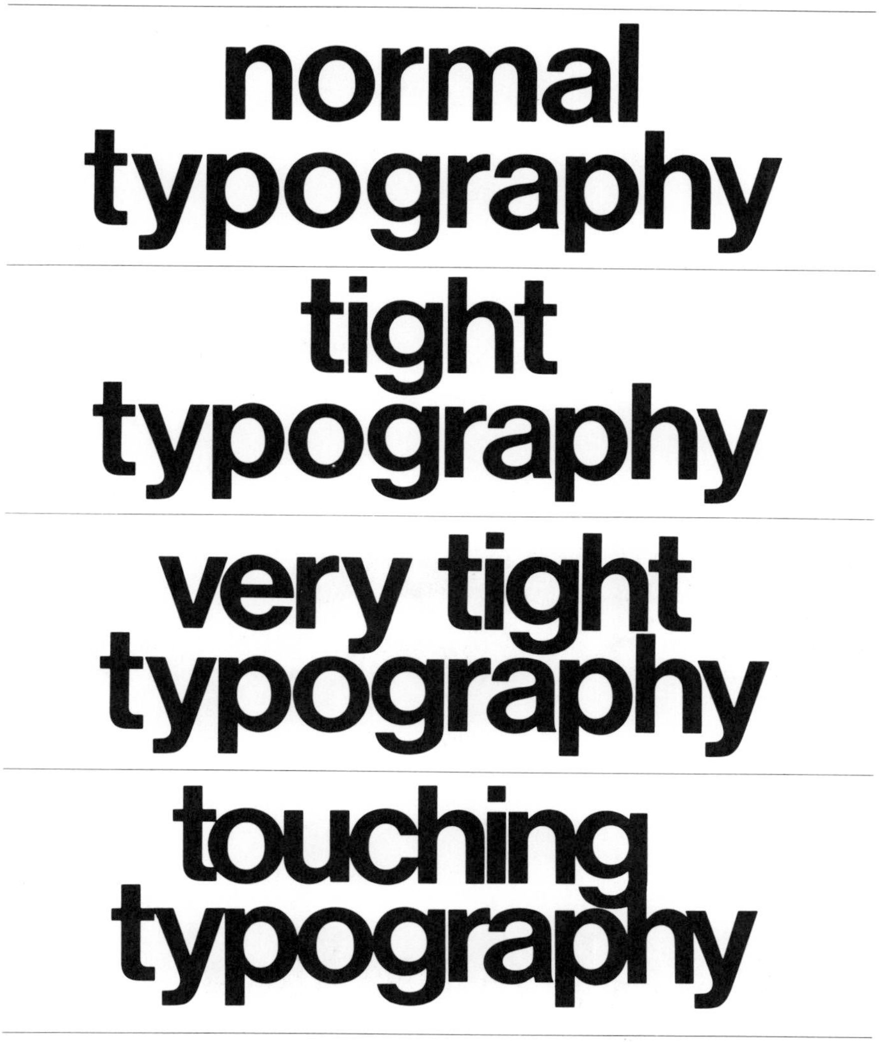

normal
typography
tight
typography
very tight
typography
touching
typography

type on the width, you will not know how high it will be. Each type face has its own proportions which must be taken into consideration.

If your layout is *comprehensively* prepared, you may order it on the height or width because those dimensions have been established. But if your layout is roughly sketched (or you have no layout at all) you must decide which dimension is more important or you may run into unexpected problems. For example, in Fig. 47 the type was ordered 2½ picas on the cap height.

The final setting is correct in type size but notice the difference in width of the line. The layout measures 32¼ picas but the type measures 36¼ picas. (The question is which is more important, the type size or the line width?)

Had it been ordered on the width it would be correct, but not 2½ picas high; Fig. 48.

Avoid disappointments by anticipating the results before ordering. For example, you might want to determine how wide or how high a line will be if set to a specific width or height. Carefully trace the copy from the alphabet specimen in your type specimen book. If the size you have traced is the correct height you will then have a fairly good idea of how wide it will be (or vice versa).

Should the traced size be larger or smaller than your requirements you can have your tracing reduced or enlarged to the proper size. There are a number of ways to do this depending upon your set up. A quick and quite reliable approach is to use the diagonal scale method.

First box in the line of type you have traced. Be sure to use a T-square and a triangle. Then draw a line from the lower left corner through the upper right corner and beyond.

Mark off the height you need. Draw a horizontal line (parallel to the base) across the designated height until it intersects the diagonal line. The point of intersection represents how wide the line will be; Fig. 49.

Fig. 47

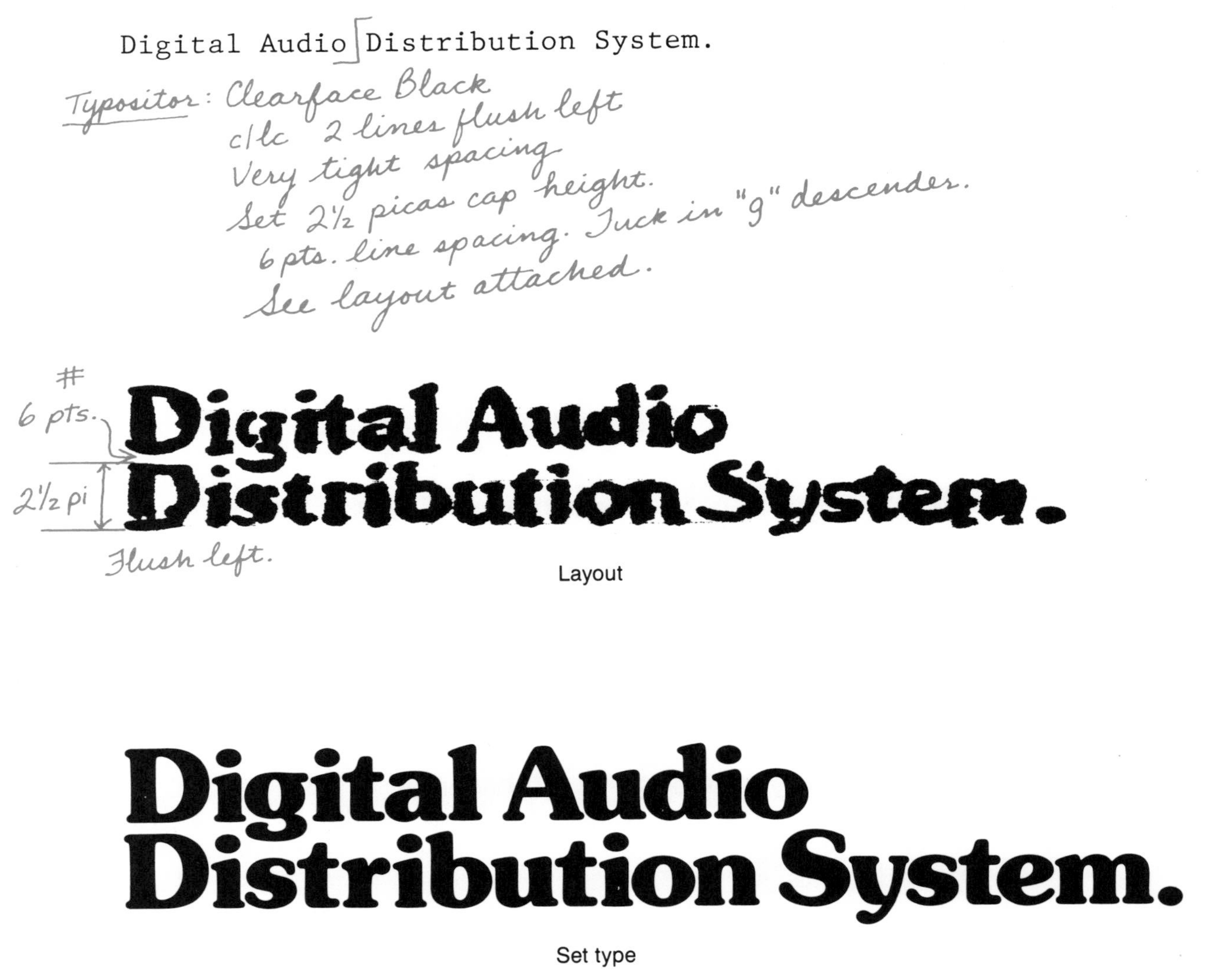

Digital Audio⌐Distribution System.

Typositor: Clearface Black
c/lc 2 lines flush left
Very tight spacing
Set 2½ picas cap height.
6 pts. line spacing. Tuck in "g" descender.
See layout attached.

#
6 pts.
2½ pi
Flush left.

Digital Audio Distribution System.

Layout

Digital Audio Distribution System.

Set type

Fig. 48

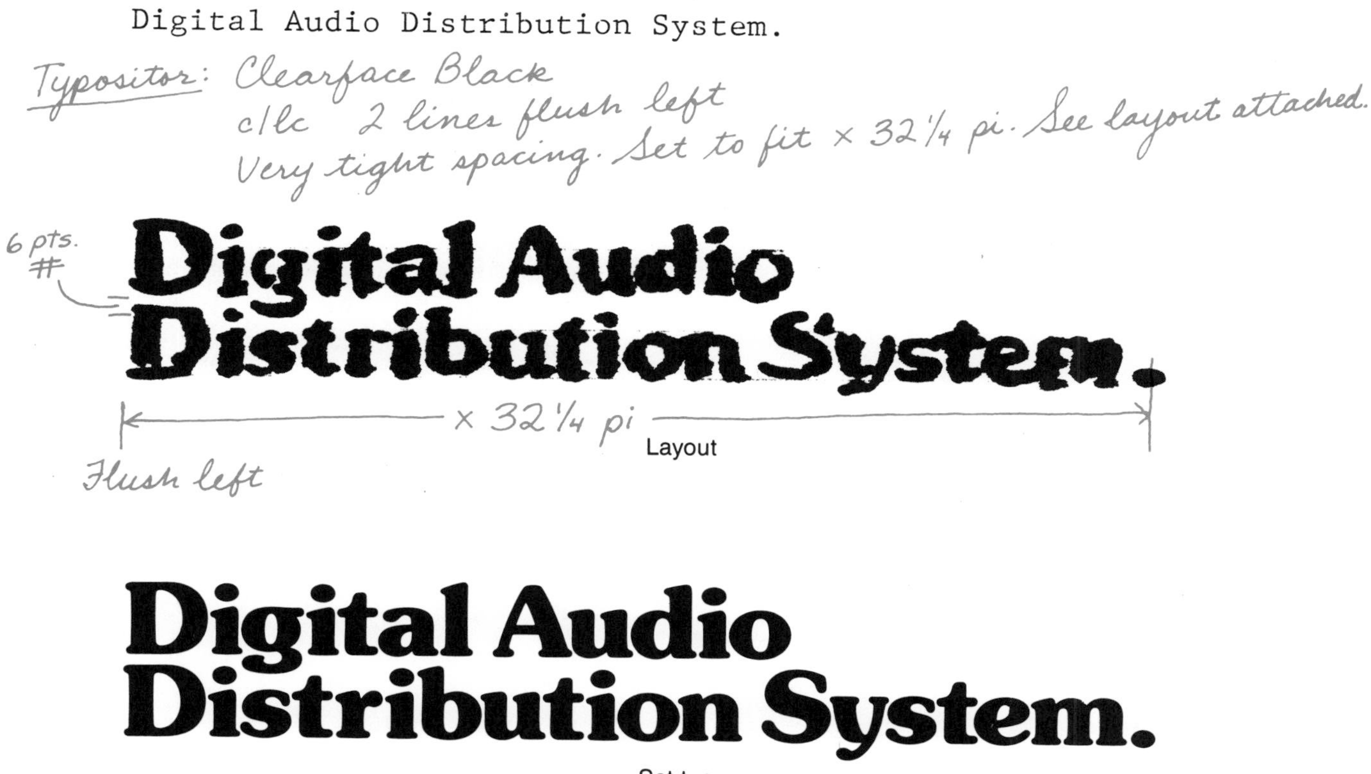

Digital Audio Distribution System.

Typositor: Clearface Black
c/lc   2 lines flush left
Very tight spacing. Set to fit × 32¼ pi. See layout attached.

6 pts.
#

Digital Audio Distribution System.

|← ———————— × 32¼ pi ———————— →|
Layout

Flush left

Digital Audio Distribution System.

Set type
Correct on the width, but not on the height

Fig. 49

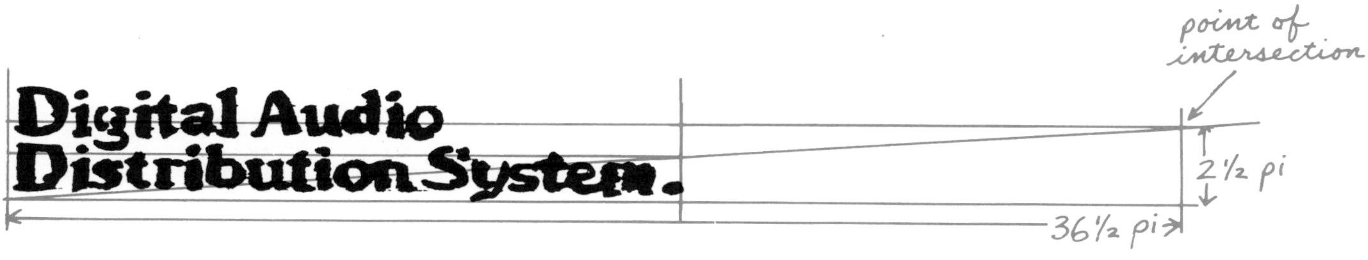

point of intersection

Digital Audio Distribution System.

2½ pi

|← ———————— 36½ pi →|

If you have decided upon the width but need to know the height just reverse the procedure. Mark off the width. Then draw a vertical line to intersect the diagonal line. That intersection represents the height.

If you have access to a photocopy machine with a zoom lens you can simply make a print of your tracing to the size you need or have the tracing *photostated* to the proper size.

If the nature of the job is such that the final decision cannot or need not be determined in advance you can order the type set to an arbitrary size. Then have the set type *photostated* to the size you need at your own discretion.

If the layout requires the type to be both a specific width and height and the face does not scale, it may be possible to have it customized by the typesetter. The type can be set to the required height and extended or condensed to the required width. It depends upon the typesetting system being used. This can be costly and should be used with discretion. Consult your typographer.

USING TEXT FACES AS HEADLINES

Many text faces offer sizes large enough to be used as headlines. Should you decide to order text type for a headline you will soon discover that it has its advantages and disadvantages.

Text type is less expensive than display type. Bear in mind that display type is charged by the word with a minimum charge as opposed to text type which is usually charged by the hour with a minimum charge.

Display typesetting normally produces only one original. If you require more than one proof you must request it in your original order.

Display heads are custom set to be esthetically pleasing, i.e. the letter spacing and size is controlled by the operator. A good typographer is a blessing.

If text type is used and enlarged for a headline it may present a letter spacing problem because the spacing is done automatically and only in some systems can be controlled by the operator. You more or less take what you get.

Refinements have to be done by hand cutting and rearranging the proof.

Some digitized text systems reproduce poorly (jagged edges) in sizes larger than 36 point.

Display heads can be composed by the typesetter to match intricate or involved layouts if required, whereas text type has its limitations to simple arrangements. While display type offers virtually no limitation to size, text type is pretty much restricted to the sizes shown in the type specimen book.

The determining factors in choosing between photo-display headlines and text type as headlines are dependent upon the requirements of the job, the time available, and of course, the budget. Display may require more time than text. For example, a headline or several headlines containing a large quantity of words may be very costly and time consuming to set in photo-display. You might alternatively set it in text type.

Chapter Six
Lists and Tables

LISTS

Type specifying a list such as a table of contents is relatively simple but does require some concentration.

As a general rule you will be facing one of two situations. You will either be asked to design a format for the layout without having the actual copy, or you will have the actual copy at the time you are designing the format.

Nevertheless when you are ready to spec the copy you have to make certain decisions. Study the layout and actual copy in Fig. 50.

This rough layout was done before the actual copy was available, so it may need to be adjusted. It is advisable that you set up your T-square and triangle so that you can prepare a tissue as you read the following basic steps.

- Count the characters in the longest line ("Chapter 8: etc." including the page number), plus at least one extra to account for the caps for a total of 46 characters.
- You have chosen 11 point Helios Light. The chart in your type book indicates 2.40 characters per pica. Divide 2.40 into 46 to get 19 picas.
- Your layout is only 17 picas wide which includes extra space between the chapter title and page number. You will have to work with a wider measure.

- If the width is to be changed you will first have to decide upon the amount of space between the title and page number. Let's say three picas. This is purely personal judgment.
- Add 3 picas to 19 which will give you the new width of 22 picas.
- The layout indicates 15 lines while the actual copy is only 10 lines deep. You will have to work with a shorter depth.
- Before determining the depth you must decide on the line spacing. Why not use 7 points making it 11/18. Once again this is a personal decision.

The gauge does not have 18 points but you can still use it by measuring 10 lines of 11 point plus 9 lines of 7 point (9 spaces between 10 lines), which measures about 14 picas. The layout indicates 21¾ picas.

- Rule a box using 14 picas for the depth and 22 picas for the width. This, now, is the total boxed in area that the type will occupy. Compare it to the layout in Fig. 50.

At this point you will have to make your own decisions. If you can visualize what these specs will look like and are confident that it will be satisfactory, then order it as such.

─── **Fig. 50** ───

Table of Contents

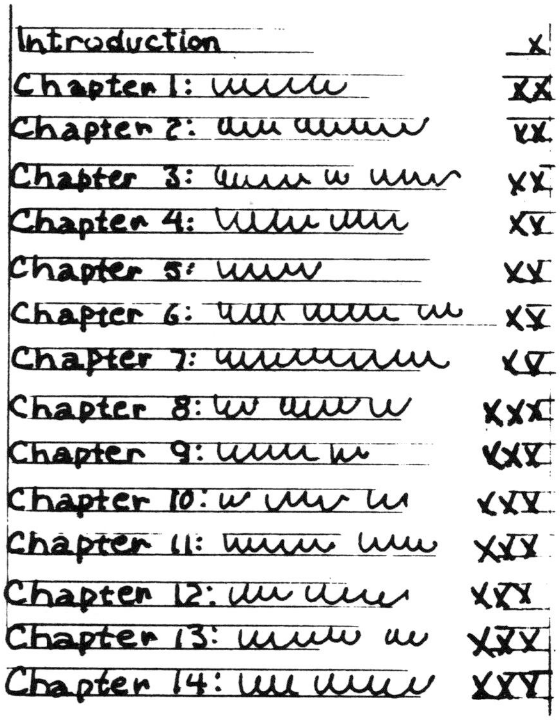

Introduction _____ x
Chapter 1: ⌣⌣⌣⌣ XX
Chapter 2: ⌣⌣ ⌣⌣⌣⌣ XX
Chapter 3: ⌣⌣⌣ ⌣ ⌣⌣⌣ XX
Chapter 4: ⌣⌣⌣ ⌣⌣⌣ XX
Chapter 5: ⌣⌣⌣ XX
Chapter 6: ⌣⌣⌣ ⌣⌣⌣⌣ ⌣⌣ XX
Chapter 7: ⌣⌣⌣⌣⌣⌣⌣⌣ XX
Chapter 8: ⌣⌣ ⌣⌣⌣⌣ ⌣ XXX
Chapter 9: ⌣⌣⌣⌣ ⌣⌣ XXX
Chapter 10: ⌣ ⌣⌣⌣ ⌣⌣ XXX
Chapter 11: ⌣⌣⌣⌣ ⌣⌣⌣ XXX
Chapter 12: ⌣⌣⌣ ⌣⌣⌣ XXX
Chapter 13: ⌣⌣⌣⌣ ⌣⌣ XXX
Chapter 14: ⌣⌣⌣ ⌣⌣⌣ XXX

Layout

Table of Contents

Actual copy

Should you need a better visualization of how it will lay out then rule up a type tissue as per your calculations.

Because the gauge does not have an 18 point slot you can make your own by ticking off 11 + 7 on the edge of a piece of paper. Use this as a gauge to mark off the lineage. You can now use these as guidelines to rough in the copy areas; Fig. 51.

Fig. 51

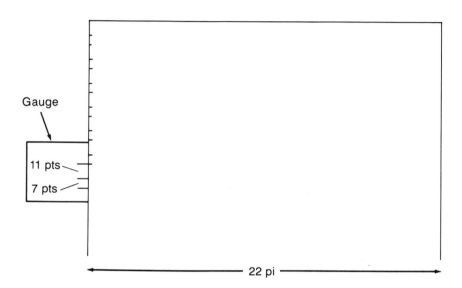

Gauge

11 pts

7 pts

22 pi

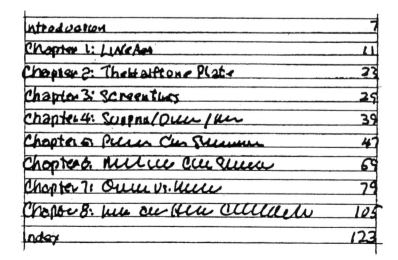

Rough layout for visualization

Your mark up and final setting would be as shown in Fig. 52.

— **Fig. 52** —

24 pt. HELVETICA LIGHT EXTENDED, c/lc

2 pi Table of Contents)
 8 pts. b/r

½ pt. rule x 24 pi

Introduction ↓ *42 pts. r/b* ——— 7

11/18 HELIOS LIGHT with FLUSH L/R x 22 pi

Chapter 1: □ Line Art ——— 11

Chapter 2: □ The Halftone Plate ——— 23

Chapter 3: □ Screen Tints ——— 29

Chapter 4: □ Surprint/Dropout/Reverse ——— 39

Chapter 5: □ Process Color Separation ——— 47

Chapter 6: □ Mechanical Color Separation ——— 59

Chapter 7: □ Overlay vs Keyline ——— 79

Set line for line

Chapter 8: □ Line and Halftone Combinations ——— 105

Index ——— 123

← x 22 pi →

Table of Contents

Introduction	**7**
Chapter 1: Line Art	**11**
Chapter 2: The Halftone Plate	**23**
Chapter 3: Screen Tints	**29**
Chapter 4: Surprint/Dropout/Reverse	**39**
Chapter 5: Process Color Separation	**47**
Chapter 6: Mechanical Color Separation	**59**
Chapter 7: Overlay vs.Keyline	**79**
Chapter 8: Line and Halftone Combinations	**105**
Index	**123**

Final setting

TABLES

A tabular setting as compared with a listing is usually more complex in format and can be quite exasperating to spec out. If ever you need to spec an annual report you'll soon realize the importance of understanding all that you have read to this point.

If you haven't been drawing and measuring the examples as you progressed, it is advisable that you do so now.

In this example which is not particularly complicated in format, you have been given the copy and must lay it out in advance in order to set it. The only restriction you have is a 35 pica width. The depth is flexible; Fig. 53.

—— **Fig. 53** ——

Increased Spending of Traditionally Strong Categories

Several traditionally heavy spending product categories have

experienced strong growth.

Category	Category Rank		Spending $(M)		% Difference
	1980	1984	1980	1984	
Beer & Ale	2	2	183,125	370,220	+102
Restaurants & Drive Ins	5	3	132,064	352,156	+166
Headache Remedies	8	6	123,644	212,648	+72
Department Stores	15	7	88,276	173,477	+97

- You have chosen 9 point Rockwell Light with medium. The first thing you need to know is how wide the copy will be in 9 point.
- Character count the manuscript by counting across the widest *lines* in each column. Do not count *spaces* between columns at this time. You want to get a solid count. Your count is 62 characters; Fig. 54.

—— **Fig. 54** ——

Increased Spending of Traditionally Strong Categories

Several traditionally heavy spending product categories have

experienced strong growth.

62

Category	Category Rank		Spending $(M)		% Difference
	1980	1984	1980	1984	
Beer & Ale	2	2	183,125	370,220	+102
Restaurants & Drive Ins	5	3	132,064	352,156	+166
Headache Remedies	8	6	123,644	212,648	+72
Department Stores	15	7	88,276	173,477	+97

- The chart for Rockwell Light in 9 point indicates 2.67 characters per pica. Convert your count of 62 into picas.

$$62 \div 2.67 = 23.22 \text{ picas}$$

The 23 picas represents the type as if it were set without space between columns. Therefore the difference between 23 picas and the full 35 pica width represents the total space available to be divided between columns.

$$35 - 23 = 12 \text{ picas space.}$$

- There are 3 column spaces. You have the option of dividing the space between each column as you see fit.

You have enough information now to construct a rough layout.

- Start by ruling two vertical lines 35 picas apart for the width. Then connect them with a double line representing the title. The space between these lines is determined by the *cap* height of 9 point type (which you know is not 9 points). Trace this out of a type book; Fig. 55.

Fig. 55

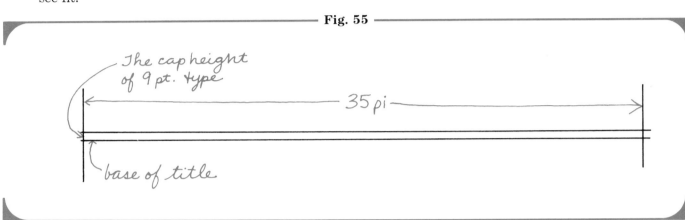

- Notice the indication for the title to be changed to all caps (Fig. 50). If you do not have a chart for caps you can use the 30% method. Remember, this is only a rough formula. The character count for the title is 53 (count them).

$$53 \div 2.67 = 19.85 \text{ picas}$$
$$19.85 + 30\% = 25.16 \text{ picas}$$

It appears that the title will fit comfortably. Roughly letter it in.

- Establish the weight and position of the rule. Let's use a 4 point rule positioned 12 points from the base of the title to the base of the rule.

- Establish the distance down from the base of the rule to the base of the subhead (14 points). These spaces are purely your judgment.
- Rule a double line to represent the subhead. It is not necessary to letter it. A quick calculation for the length of this line would be 86 characters, (count them,) divided by 2.67 to equal 32 picas. It will fit.
- The column heads can be positioned 22 points base to base below the subhead. You might rough in the first column head to pinpoint your position within the layout; Fig. 56.

Fig. 56

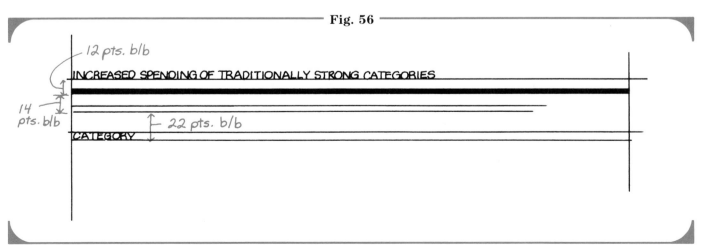

- We'll use 9/11 as line spacing. Position your gauge at the base of the column head using the 11 slot and tick off 5 lines representing the text. Draw guide lines through these marks to the 35 pica width; Fig. 57.

──── **Fig. 57** ────

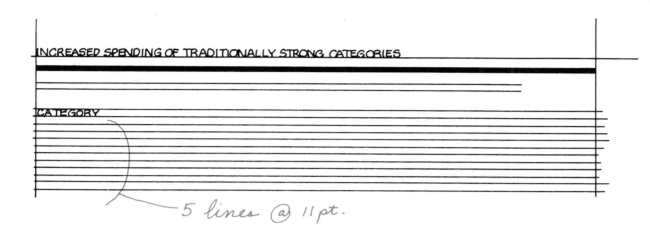

INCREASED SPENDING OF TRADITIONALLY STRONG CATEGORIES

CATEGORY

— 5 lines @ 11 pt.

- Using this basic guide you can now sketch in whatever you feel is necessary to visualize the format. This can be done by eye rather than character counting each line to more or less position the columns; Fig. 58.

──── **Fig. 58** ────

INCREASED SPENDING OF TRADITIONALLY STRONG CATEGORIES

| CATEGORY | CATEGORY RANK | SPENDING $ (M) | % DIFFERENCE |

- Mark up the copy according to your calculations and this layout. Send both to the typesetter. Study the type specs in Fig. 59.

——— **Fig. 59** ———

Type specifications

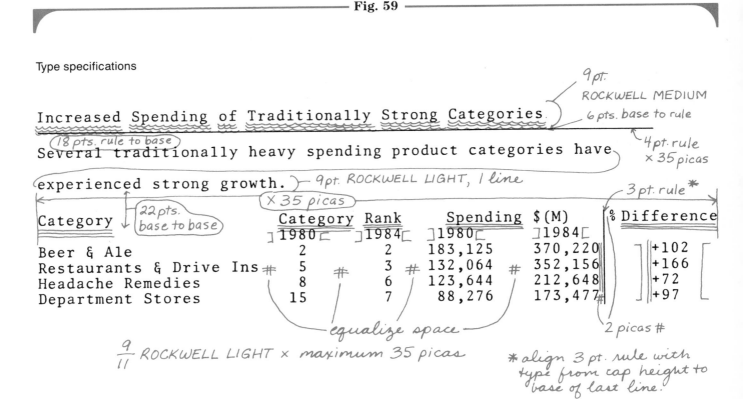

9 pt.
ROCKWELL MEDIUM
6 pts. base to rule

Increased Spending of Traditionally Strong Categories.

18 pts. rule to base

Several traditionally heavy spending product categories have

4 pt. rule
× 35 picas

experienced strong growth. ⟩— 9pt. ROCKWELL LIGHT, I line

× 35 picas

3 pt. rule *

22 pts.
base to base

Category	Category Rank		Spending $ (M)		% Difference
	1980	1984	1980	1984	
Beer & Ale	2	2	183,125	370,220	+102
Restaurants & Drive Ins	5	3	132,064	352,156	+166
Headache Remedies	8	6	123,644	212,648	+72
Department Stores	15	7	88,276	173,477	+97

equalize space

2 picas #

9/11 ROCKWELL LIGHT × maximum 35 picas

* align 3 pt. rule with type from cap height to base of last line.

INCREASED SPENDING OF TRADITIONALLY STRONG CATEGORIES

Several traditionally heavy spending product categories have experienced strong growth.

CATEGORY	CATEGORY RANK		SPENDING $ (M)		% DIFFERENCE
	1980	1984	1980	1984	
Beer & Ale	2	2	183,125	370,220	+102
Restaurants & Drive Ins	5	3	132,064	352,156	+166
Headache Remedies	8	6	123,644	212,648	+72
Department Stores	15	7	88,276	173,477	+97

Final setting

Chapter Seven
The Brochure

The term brochure usually calls to mind the thought of a pamphlet or booklet consisting of four to as many as sixty-four pages or more, averaging between twelve and thirty-six pages. Its page size may vary but is usually a standard 8½ × 11″ and is saddle stitched (stapled in the center fold).

Designing and type specifying a brochure is only as simple or complex as the elements it is to contain. The average components would be headlines, subheads, body copy, photo captions, tables, charts, art and photos. This is not to say that all brochures contain each of these elements. It depends upon the nature of the subject. An annual report, for example, which is essentially a brochure, might include all of them.

HOW TO SPEC A 12-PAGE BROCHURE

Before you can type spec a brochure it must be designed, taking into account all the elements. Designing and type specifying in this instance are decidedly interrelated. While there is no set formula for this kind of project the following is a general approach that many artists use. It is one that incorporates both the mechanics of type specification and general layout. Because the esthetic decisions are personal and this is a lesson in type specification,

we will condense the progression until we reach those stages requiring decisions in typography.

This corporate brochure will contain eleven 2¼ × 2¼″ color transparencies, three tabular charts and 7 pages of manuscript. The page size is 8½ × 11″. Our budget limits us to eight text pages, plus cover (a twelve page brochure).

Start by assembling all the material. Spread it out, coordinate the units. Become familiar with the photos, their content, proportion and relative importance. Establish the sequence of the material. A review of the manuscript reveals that it consists of cover copy, table of contents, introduction, running narrative (text or body copy), major headings, subheads, captions for the photos, and tabular charts.

Its contents will be made up of three sections. The overall description of the company; product photos, related charts, company procedure photos, descriptive captions; and summary copy. Let's get started.

Prepare a down-sized thumbnail storyboard recording all the components by roughly indicating the general sequence and location of elements, approximating the amount of space each will occupy. This is done without conscious effort for design. You are simply organizing your thoughts or "getting into the job"; Fig. 60.

Fig. 60

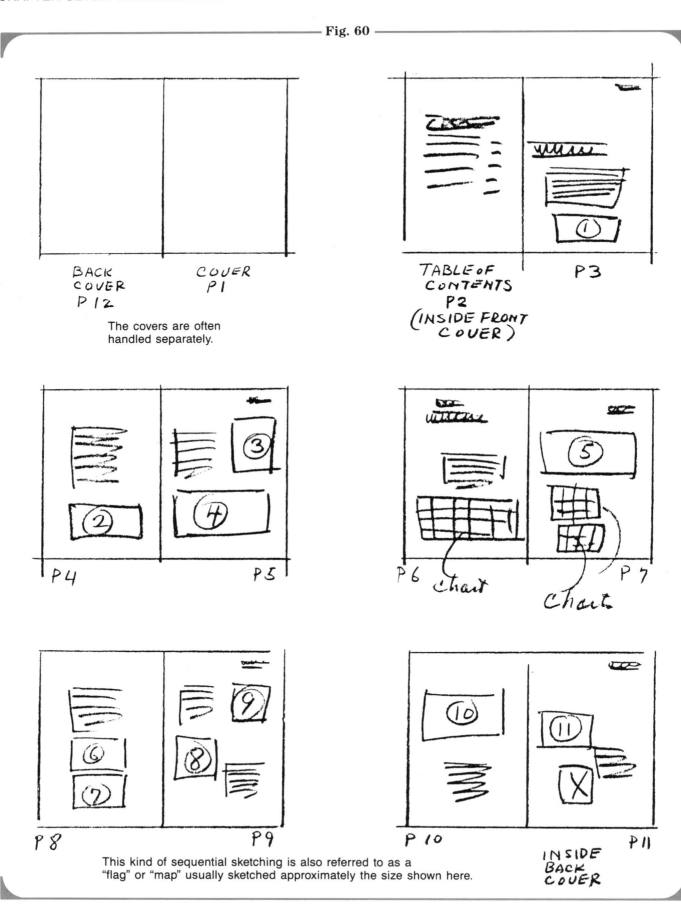

BACK COVER P 12

COUER P 1

The covers are often handled separately.

TABLE OF CONTENTS P2 (INSIDE FRONT COUER)

P 3

P 4

P 5

P 6 Chart

P 7 Chart

P 8

P 9

P 10

P 11

INSIDE BACK COUER

This kind of sequential sketching is also referred to as a "flag" or "map" usually sketched approximately the size shown here.

Keep in mind that at this phase of the project you may not be certain that the material you have to work with will fit 12 pages. But because of your past experience with this kind of job, you will have developed an instinct that tells you whether or not it will fit.

Now you can make additional thumbnail sketches developing a page format and design, tightening each sketch as you progress, still only approximating the space occupied by both text and photos. Once you have established the look you want it is time to begin more accurate sketches.

Until now you have simply indicated text blocks but not type face and size. Most of what you do from now on might be subject to change later on but you must start somewhere.

Prepare an actual size master "template" (guide) to be used for both design and type specification of each page. This is done in order to establish definite dimensions of components and specific format (design) restrictions such as column widths, margins, etc. This is purely your own artistic decision; Fig. 61.

— **Fig. 61** —

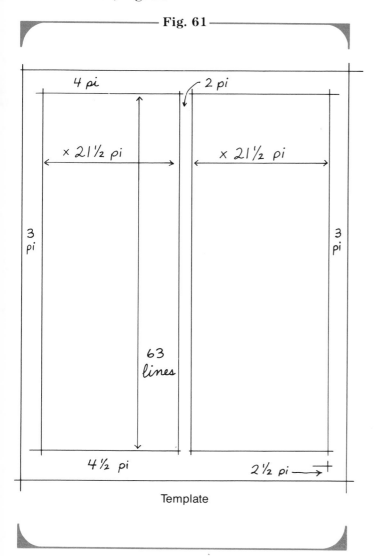

Template

We have reached that aspect of the project which might be subject to criticism by many designers.

You can continue refining your layout and design without consideration for the actual proportion of the photos or the actual space the copy will in fact occupy after it has been set. Many designers prefer to "eyeball" the shapes and spaces of photos and type blocks for the sake of design. This of course, lifts all restrictions and make it a lot easier to develop a pleasing design. But be careful. This approach requires considerable experience. You run the risk of having a design approved only to discover that you cannot adhere to it because the photos do not scale properly or the copy doesn't convert to type the way you designed it.

Until you have developed such expertise, it might be wise to follow this philosophy. It is best to know exactly what you have to work with in terms of size, proportion and quantity. There is little time for surprises at the final production stage. Scale your photos and spec the copy as you design. When you are finished you will have designed a brochure that can be produced the way you want it.

Using the template as a guide, trace off the dimensions onto tissue paper, page for page, to be used for your calculations in blocking out the text.

Count out the manuscript so that you can determine how much total space the copy will occupy. You can do this item for item, page for page, as you have laid it out in the rough sketches.

It is too soon to work out the table of contents. This is generally done after the entire book has been developed. Start with page three or the first page of text. This is a simple enough page containing only one paragraph. Ignore the headline at this time. You'll want to take time later on to determine face and size.

Your character count for this paragraph should be around 410 characters. Make a note of it in pencil alongside the paragraph for reference if needed later on; Fig. 62.

Choice of text face is generally your design decision. The average designer seldom works with more than four or five text faces that he feels comfortable with. Our choice for this book is Century Expanded.

According to your template, the column width is 21.5 picas. The question is how much space will be needed for the copy? You must now select the type size but bear in mind that the size you select will be used throughout the book and must fit each page. It is not advisable from a standpoint of design to mix text sizes unless it serves a specific purpose such as special emphasis or a caption. However the structure of this layout is open enough that the size should not present a problem. The average text size is 9 point but 9 point Century Expanded seems small so let's use 10 point. Take your calculator, pencil, scrap paper, and layout sheet, and begin.

The copy consists of 410 characters. The chart for 10 point Century Expanded indicates 56 characters to one line of 21.5 picas. Divide 56 into 410 to get 8 lines. Your

---
— **Fig. 62** —

Page 3

The Latest in Technology

Tomac, Inc. has been a leading supplier of quality
components and subsystems for the industry since 1972.
The company's products cover the entire spectrum of
applications involving the generation, amplification,
detection, and control of microwave energy. They are
installed in a variety of military and commercial
systems, in conjunction with radar, missile guidance
electronics, and communications hardware.

343
26
41
410

(Caption
for photo)

Tomac maintains extensive research
development and production facilities
at its ultra-modern headquarters
complex in Hampton, XY. Other offices
and facilities are located throughout
the world.

160
23
9
192

Page 4

Quality Products

Throughout its existence, Tomac, Inc. has consistently
maintained the highest levels of reliability, performance,
and cost effectiveness in its product development and
manufacturing operations. Coupling this policy with a
regular program of internal growth and selective acquisition,
the company has reached a point where it can now demonstrate
a unique capacity for designing, building, and integrating
the most comprehensive line of microwave components and
subsystems in the industry.

432
30
27
489

The latest expression of this capability involves the
development of an extensive new line of millimeter wave
products. Produced by the company's Millimeter Wave Division,
this line consists of four basic segments which include
standard components, subsystems, advanced components and
high frequency devices.

270
18
23
311

Standard components consist of mixers, detectors, converters,
and oscillators in popular frequency bands. Subsystems range
from custom designed units, in bolted-together configurations,
to packages that are creatively designed to accommodate special
form factors. The third segment, consisting of supercomponents,
involves specially-built packages where many complex functions
are integrated to produce units that are capable of meeting
superior performance standards.

378
63
31
472

(Caption
for photo)

Tomac manufactures a complete line of
standard millimeter wave devices and
component systems.

93

calculations conclude that the first page of text will be 8 lines deep.

Rule a line across the layout tissue you have drawn establishing the position of the first line of type. You have decided to set it 10/11, flush left, rag right on a maximum of 21.5 picas. Box in the width and mark off 8 lines of 11. You now know exactly how much space you will need for the copy. How you *arrange* it is purely up to your descretion. But you are not ready for final layout at this time. You are simply establishing the size of the type blocks; Fig. 63.

Continue calculating the rest of the copy in the same manner, one paragraph at a time. The copy for the next page is "Quality Products." The first paragraph counts out to a total of 489 characters. The second is 311, and the third is 472. Once again, convert the totals into lines by dividing each by 56.

Paragraph one equals 9 lines. Paragraph two equals 6 lines. Paragraph three equals 9 lines, for a total of 24 lines.

By now you should give some though to how you will treat the subheads. It isn't necessary to spec them, but they can be roughly indicated as you go along.

Because the logo must also appear on each spread you can at this time combine these elements with your calculations. Do the same for page five; Fig. 64.

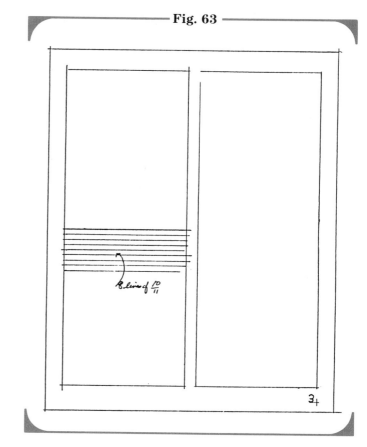

Fig. 63

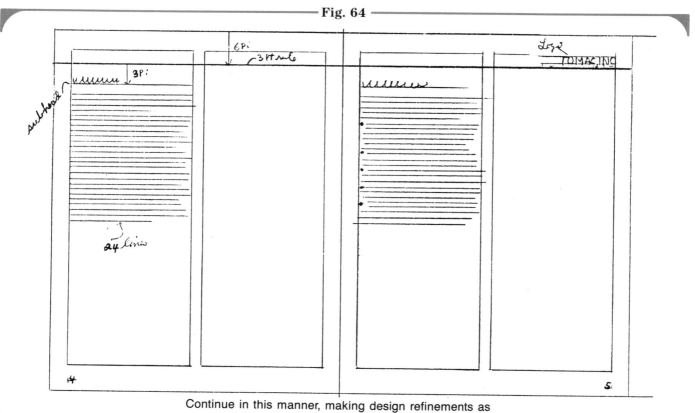

Fig. 64

Continue in this manner, making design refinements as you progress, until all the copy has been indicated.

Repeat this procedure with each paragraph in the manuscript recording your calculations on your layout sheet. Skip the charts (p. 6 & 7) for the time being as they will take more time and work. You want to develop the text pages first. Be sure to keep notes of your math, character count totals, lineage, point sizes, etc. You may find it necessary to go back over a page to recalculate for one reason or another. Your notes will save time. Certainly you will need to refer to them when you are ready to mark up the manuscript to send to the typographer for typesetting.

Once you have calculated the space needed for all the text, you can proceed to develop a more definite layout incorporating both text and photos.

Do not forget to scale the photos. You need to know exactly how much space they will require and how they will relate to the text and their captions (which you have yet to work out).

Once you have organized your pages and feel confident that you have the design under control, you can select a type face for the heads and indicate the captions; Fig.65.

Fig. 65 A

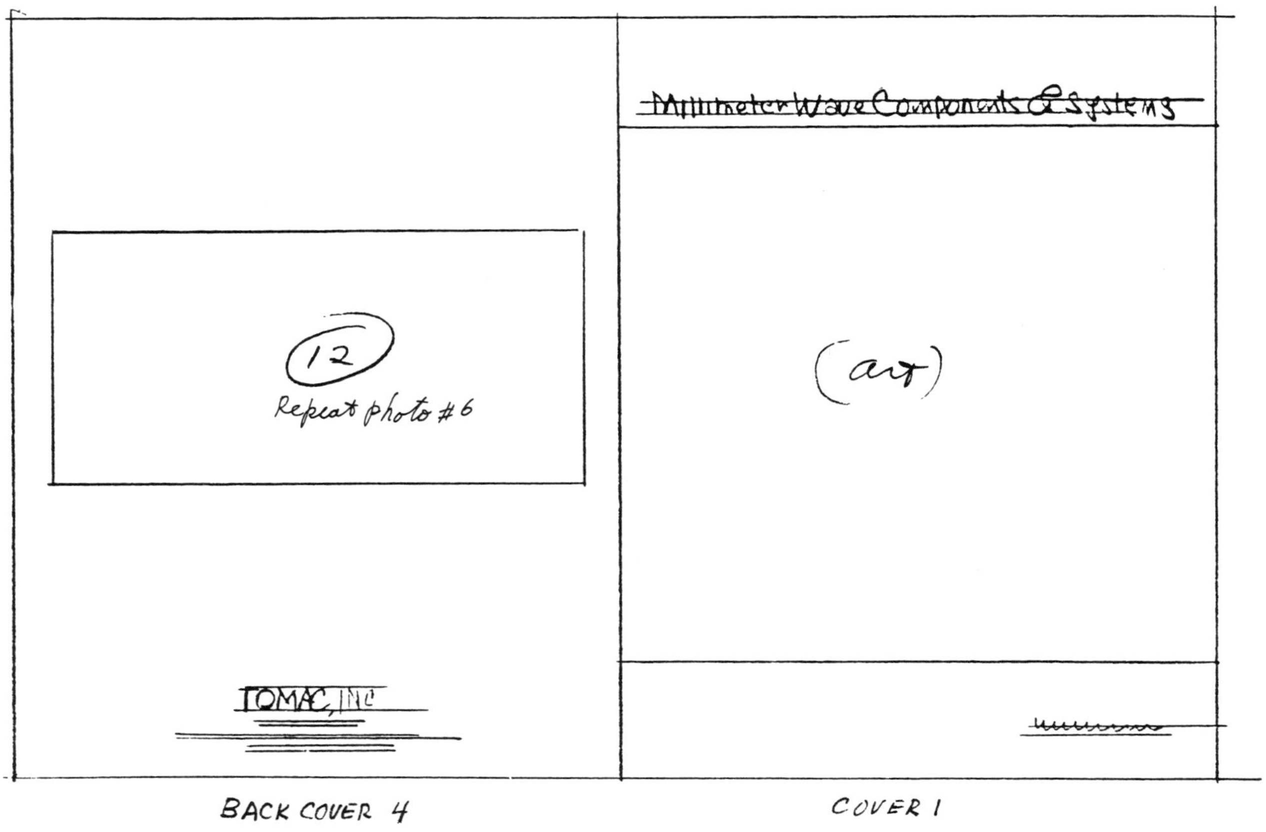

BACK COVER 4

COVER 1

Fig. 65B

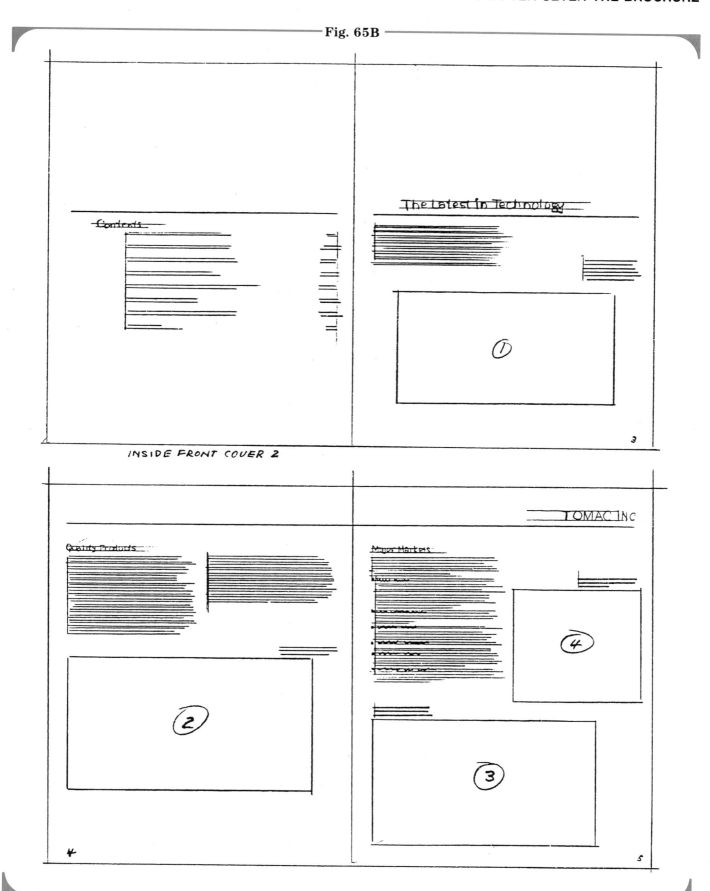

Fig. 65C

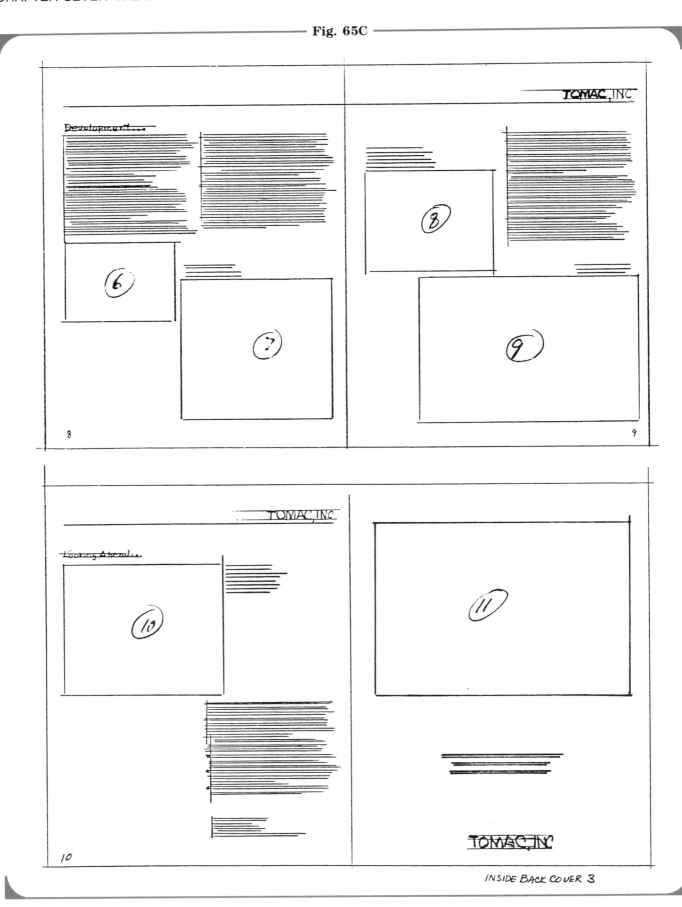

These layouts represent your first approach to the continuity of your design. It will be refined and personalized after you have calculated the entire book. The important thing at this time is that you now know the sizes of all components and have determined whether or not you will have problem areas to contend with.

Let's take a look at the tables; Fig. 66.

─── **Fig. 66** ───

9006
converters   IF inputs   TOMAC INC.(LOGO)

BAND DESIGNATION	K	A	B	U	V	E	W
FREQUENCY (GHz)	18–26.5	26.5–40	33–50	40–50	50–75	60–90	75–110
WAVEGUIDE	WR–42	WR–28	WR–22	WR–19	WR–15	WR–12	WR–10
MODEL NUMBER	K9600U	A9600U	B9600U	U9600U	V9600U	E9600U	W9600U
IF INPUT RANGE	10–1000 MHz	10–1000 MHz	10–1000 MHz	10–1000 MHz	10–1000 MHz	10–1000 MHz	100–1000 MHz
CONVERSION LOSS (dB)	8.0	8.0	8.5	8.5	9.0	9.5	10.0

IF INPUT BANDWIDTH	DESIGNATOR
10–110 MHz	–02
100–600 MHz	–05
100–1000 MHz	–09
1000–2000 MHz	–13
2000–4000 MHz	–19
4000–8000 MHz	–14
Special	TBD

GENERAL RATINGS	
RF Bandwidth	Up to 5 GHz
Conversion	= 1dB Type
LO Input Power	+ 10 dBm.Max
IF Input Power	+ 20 dBm.Max
RF Output Power	+ 8 dBm.Min
LO VSWR	2.0 Max
IF VSWR	2.0 Max
LO/RF	21 Db.Min
Operating Temperature	0°C to 66°C
Storage Temperature	–55°C to +110°C

You have two facing pages into which you must incorporate three charts, text copy, a product photo, and a title. Before you start calculations it might be best to refer back to your initial thumbnail sketch and redraw a more definite layout (actual size), approximating the size and placement of each element; Fig. 67.

Fig. 67

Thumbnail this size.

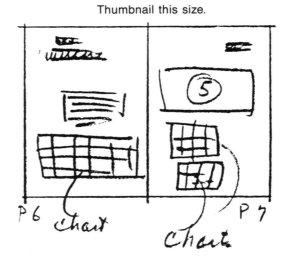

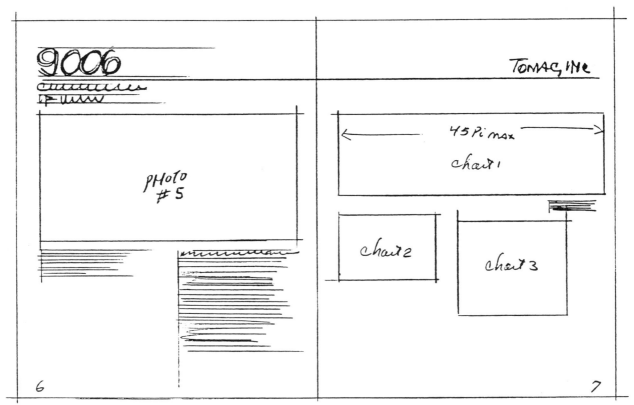

Actual size: 11″ x 17″.

With this layout you have a starting point for the type calculation. Let's see if you can get it to work.

Count the largest chart first. You need to know how wide and deep it will be when set in type. But should you use Century for this? Here is where you use your discretion and consider a different type face. Perhaps a less decorative, simple face would be easier to read. Let's use Helios Light.

You'll notice that 10 point Helios Light appears to be larger than 10 point Century, whereas the 9 point specimen seems to be large enough and we'll get a better line count. So let's try it. Study the chart and count the *widest line (or combination of lines)* across.

You'll have to include space between groups. A minimum of 2 em space on either side of the rules is a good guide; Fig. 68.

Fig. 68

9006
converters   IF inputs   TOMAC INC. (LOGO)

BAND DESIGNATION	K	A	B	U	V	E	W
FREQUENCY (GHz)	18–26.5	26.5–40	33–50	40–50	50–75	60–90	75–110
WAVEGUIDE	WR–42	WR–28	WR–22	WR–19	WR–15	WR–12	WR–10
MODEL NUMBER	K9600U	A9600U	B9600U	U9600U	V9600U	E9600U	W9600U
IF INPUT RANGE	10–1000 MHz	10–1000 MHz	10–1000 MHz	10–1000 MHz	10–1000 MHz	10–1000 MHz	100–1000 MHz
CONVERSION LOSS (dB)	8.0	8.0	8.5	8.5	9.0	9.5	10.0

IF INPUT BANDWIDTH	DESIGNATOR
10–110 MHz	–02
100–600 MHz	–05
100–1000 MHz	–09
1000–2000 MHz	–13
2000–4000 MHz	–19
4000–8000 MHz	–14
Special	TBD

GENERAL RATINGS	
RF Bandwidth	Up to 5 GHz
Conversion	= 1dB Type
LO Input Power	+ 10 dBm.Max
IF Input Power	+ 20 dBm.Max
RF Output Power	+ 8 dBm.Min
LO VSWR	2.0 Max
IF VSWR	2.0 Max
LO/RF	21 Db.Min
Operating Temperature	0°C to 66°C
Storage Temperature	–55°C to +110°C

While calculating, keep in mind that you have a maximum 45 pica width. The total count across is 101 characters. Your chart for 9 point Helios will show 2.93 characters per pica.

$$101 \div 2.93 = 35 \text{ picas}$$

You'll have no trouble fitting it into 45 picas.

Now for the depth. The table consists of 6 categories but 7 lines. You'll need space above and below. Six points above and below should prove to be readable.

Add all the lines and spaces.
- Mark off 7 lines of 9 point on your scale.
- Add to that 6 picas (12 spaces of 6 points).
- The total equals 11¼ picas.

Your overall measurement is 45 picas by approximately 11¼ picas deep.

Now do the same for chart two. The width is 36 characters. Divide by 2.93 (12¼ picas).

The depth is 8 lines of 9 point.

Plus 16 spaces of 6 points (8 picas) equals 14 picas.

The overall dimensions are 12¼ picas wide by approximately 14 picas deep.

As for the third chart . . . why don't *you* calculate it?

You have enough information to suggest a layout. All you need to do at this point is box in the table areas.

It is time to select a face and size for the heads. Although there aren't many in this book they are probably one of the most influential elements of your overall design. Your choice of type face, size and placement is critical to the balance, continuity and attitude of the entire book.

You have decided that Century Ultra Condensed would offer a pleasing contrast to the text. Return now to page 3 and make a rough sketch of the size and placement for the headline you feel works with that page. Check your sketch against the specimen in your type book to decide on the size that comes closest. Then count the characters and measure it against the type book until you find the size appropriate for this page.

Your treatment for the chart spread may be entirely different. Perhaps a broader, bolder element is needed to add some life to it. Your approach to this is the same as for the headlines. Consult your display type face specimens and decide on faces and sizes, measuring and calculating as you go until you find something that fits and looks right to you.

That's it! Count, measure, calculate and decide. Now that you know the sizes and shapes of every element to be used you can prepare more refined layouts; Fig. 69.

Once you have developed a final layout and it has been approved for setting, you can refer to your notes and mark up the copy, confident that it will all fit as you designed it.

Your type specifications for the text, heads, captions and charts would be as shown in Fig. 70A&B.

Fig. 69

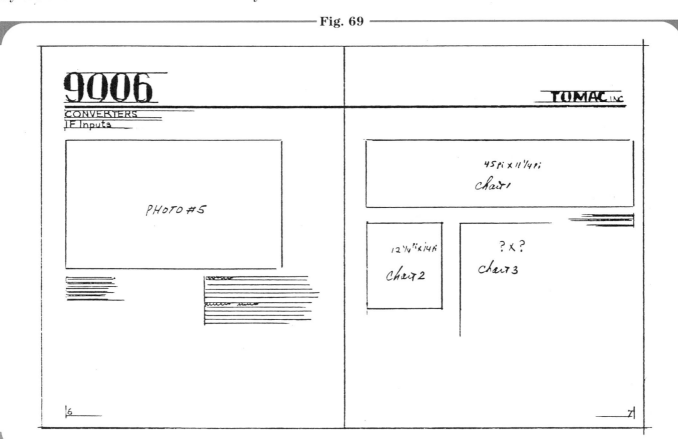

Fig. 70A

(Page 3) — I.D.

The Latest in Technology) — 30pt. CENTURY ULTRA CONDENSED c/lc (PATCH)

CUTTING

10/11 CENTURY EXPANDED, Flush left, rag right x maximum 21½ picas

TIGHT RAG; NO HYPHENS

Tomac, Inc. has been a leading supplier of quality components and subsystems for the industry since 1972. The company's products cover the entire spectrum of applications involving the generation, amplification, detection, and control of microwave energy. They are installed in a variety of military and commercial systems, in conjunction with radar, missile guidance electronics, and communications hardware.

(Caption for photo) — DNS

CUTTING

Tomac maintains extensive research development and production facilities at its ultra-modern headquarters complex in Hampton, XY. Other offices and facilities are located throughout the world.

7/8 HELVETICA Fl. left, rag right x maximum 10 picas

(Page 4) — I.D.

CUTTING

Quality Products) — 16pt. CENTURY ULTRA CONDENSED, c/lc FL. LEFT with TEXT BELOW

(18 pts. b/b)

Throughout its existence, Tomac, Inc. has consistently maintained the highest levels of reliability, performance, and cost effectiveness in its product development and manufacturing operations. Coupling this policy with a regular program of internal growth and selective acquisition, the company has reached a point where it can now demonstrate a unique capacity for designing, building, and integrating the most comprehensive line of microwave components and subsystems in the industry.
☐ The latest expression of this capability involves the development of an extensive new line of millimeter wave products. Produced by the company's Millimeter Wave Division, this line consists of four basic segments which include standard components, subsystems, advanced components and high frequency devices.
☐ Standard components consist of mixers, detectors, converters, and oscillators in popular frequency bands. Subsystems range from custom designed units, in bolted-together configurations, to packages that are creatively designed to accommodate special form factors. The third segment, consisting of supercomponents, involves specially-built packages where many complex functions are integrated to produce units that are capable of meeting superior performance standards.

10/11 CENTURY EXPANDED, Flush left, rag right x maximum 21½ picas

TIGHT RAG; NO HYPHENS

(Caption for photo) — I.D.

CUTTING

Tomac manufactures a complete line of standard millimeter wave devices and component systems.

7/8 HELVETICA Fl. left, rag right x maximum 10 picas

Fig. 70B

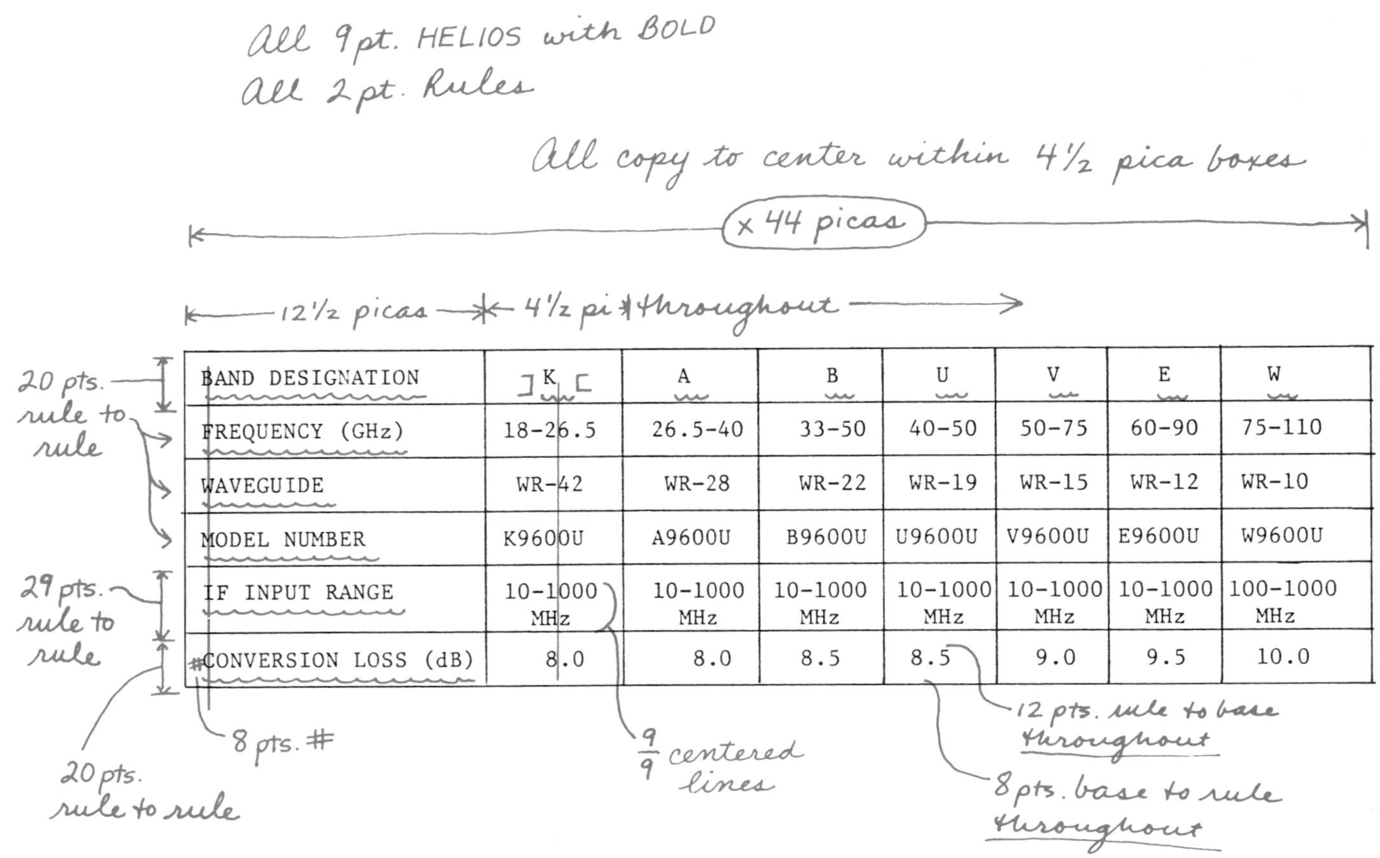

All 9pt. HELIOS with BOLD
All 2pt. Rules

All copy to center within 4½ pica boxes

⟨× 44 picas⟩

|←——— 12½ picas ———→|← 4½ pi throughout ——————→|

20 pts.
rule to
rule

BAND DESIGNATION	⌉K⌊	A	B	U	V	E	W
FREQUENCY (GHz)	18-26.5	26.5-40	33-50	40-50	50-75	60-90	75-110
WAVEGUIDE	WR-42	WR-28	WR-22	WR-19	WR-15	WR-12	WR-10
MODEL NUMBER	K9600U	A9600U	B9600U	U9600U	V9600U	E9600U	W9600U
IF INPUT RANGE	10-1000 MHz	10-1000 MHz	10-1000 MHz	10-1000 MHz	10-1000 MHz	10-1000 MHz	100-1000 MHz
#CONVERSION LOSS (dB)	8.0	8.0	8.5	8.5	9.0	9.5	10.0

29 pts.
rule to
rule

8 pts. #

20 pts.
rule to rule

9/9 centered lines

12 pts. rule to base throughout

8 pts. base to rule throughout

End Result

BAND DESIGNATION	K	A	B	U	V	E	W
FREQUENCY (GHz)	18-26.5	26.5-40	33-50	40-50	50-75	60-90	75-110
WAVEGUIDE	WR-42	WR-28	WR-22	WR-19	WR-15	WR-12	WR-10
MODEL NUMBER	K9600U	A9600U	B9600U	U9600U	V9600U	E9600U	W9600U
IF INPUT RANGE	10-1000 MHz	10-1000 MHz	10-1000 MHz	10-1000 MHz	10-1000 MHz	10-1000 MHz	100-1000 MHz
CONVERSION LOSS (dB)	8.0	8.0	8.5	8.5	9.0	9.5	10.0

Chapter Eight
Books, Books & More Books

HOW TO DETERMINE A PAGE COUNT

Before setting type for a book manuscript, you may need to estimate the number of pages it will convert into. A continuous text such as a novel is probably the simplest to specify, whereas a manuscript, interrupted with illustrations, photos, examples, etc., could be more involved. In either case, if the manuscript is not properly typed and organized, it could be chaotic.

Let's consider a continuous manuscript for a novel and let's say that it has been *ideally* typed with each page having the same number of lines and approximately the same width. The approach is academic. You simply calculate the number of characters in one page using the standard formula for character counting, then multiply the total characters for one page by the total number of manuscript pages.

The total could be staggering. For example, if one page total is 1,456 characters and you have 250 manuscript pages, the grand total would be around 364,000 characters. This may seem like a lot but when converted to type set pages it really isn't much.

If the type face and size to be used equals 55 characters per line and the page depth is 43 lines then 55×43 equals 2,365 characters per page. Divide 2,365 into 364,000 (total manuscript characters) to equal 154 pages. Simple? *Only* under *ideal* conditions.

I seriously doubt that your will ever work with a perfect manuscript as just described. At best, it will consist of full pages, partial pages and revised pages, inserts, and some pages typed wider or narrower than the others—and if different typewriters were used it really gets sticky.

For this typical manuscript the formula application is the same but requires more work. You'll have to divide the manuscript into as many groups (full pages, partial pages, etc.) as necessary and calculate each separately, then add them for the grand total. It takes a bit of patience but it can be done. You must also remember that you are only estimating. Do not expect the type to set to the exact number of pages calculated. It can be off by several pages more or less depending upon the nature of the manuscript. You are simply trying to approximate the number of pages the book will contain.

If it is essential that you work up a more accurate count, the best approach would be to have 4 or 5 manuscript pages actually set. The *setting* can then be used as a gauge. For example if five manuscript pages produce three type set pages you have a ratio of 3 to 5. A 250 page manuscript might convert to 150 type set pages.

If the manuscript contains illustrations you might estimate the approximate total number of pages they will occupy and add it to the number of estimated type pages to acquire a grand total. This also is only an approximation. The nature of the manuscript has much to do with determining the total pages.

A helpful approach (time permitting) is to prepare a storyboard layout calculating the type areas and illustrations page for page. This can easily be done in a "scaled down" size rather than actual size. You might work a ½ size scale, simply dividing all the dimensions in half.

For example, if the page size is 8⅛ × 9⅛, rule a shape 4-1/16 × 4-9/16. If the type area is 42 picas wide by 46 picas deep it will be 21 × 23 on your storyboard, etc.; Fig. 71.

Fig. 71

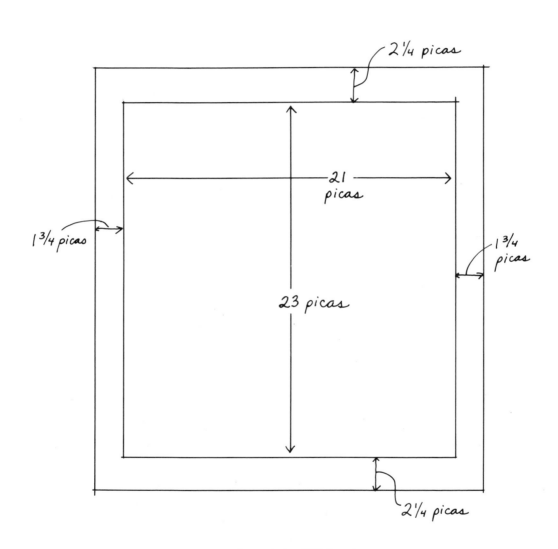

Layout size (1/2 down)

If you have access to photocopy equipment you can rule up a master spread and make as many copies as you might need. Using these miniature page forms you can develop your page design while determining the page count.

For example, if the type area is to be 10/11 you'll see that 46 picas equals 50 lines of 11. Therefore, when using the 11 scale on the storyboard each unit of 11 will equal 2 lines. It may seem confusing at first but you'll get the hang of it soon enough. Here is how it would work using a standard layout of running text interrupted by art:

- Calculate and estimate the number of lines in the manuscript up to the point where it is to be interrupted by art. Let's say 70 lines.
- Using the 11 scale mark off 25 lines on the first page and 10 lines on the second page.
- Estimate the area you'll need for the art. Remember to divide it in half. If the art area requires 16 picas of depth then mark off 8 picas on the layout; Fig. 72.

Continue counting the text until the next interruption, which may be only a few lines further on or several pages. At any rate, this is the essence of how it is done. By the time you have done three or four pages you will begin to gain control of the manuscript. Of course, you will have to make many adjustments as you progress, but you'll find this to be quite a useful method. Don't forget the "front matter."

You must realize that this procedure is not meant to be a precise calculation. It is only an approximation to be used in the preliminary stage of production and design. You need a general idea of the overall length of the book before you start production. When you are ready to go into production you will probably set type (reader's proofs) and prepare a dummy.

—— **Fig. 72** ——

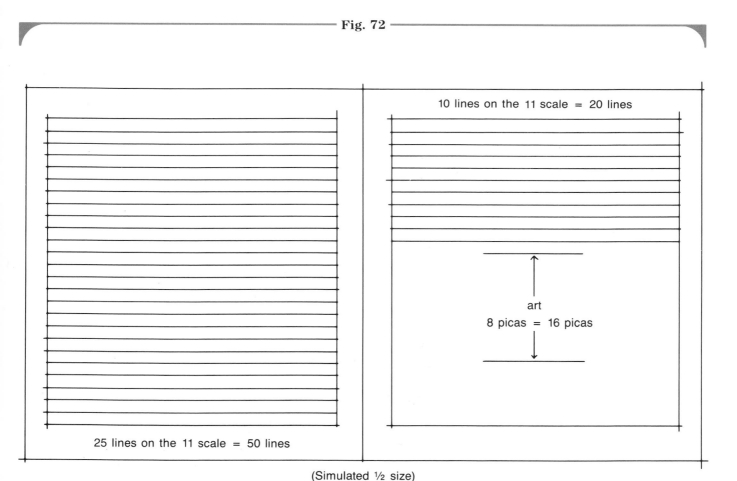

10 lines on the 11 scale = 20 lines

art
8 picas = 16 picas

25 lines on the 11 scale = 50 lines

(Simulated ½ size)

MARKING UP THE MANUSCRIPT

Once you have established most of your specifications and decided upon a format, the next step would be to have sample pages set. This will be the true look of the page giving you the opportunity to fine tune the layout. The sample pages are also used for editorial and design approval *before* releasing the entire manuscript. It is not uncommon to have sample pages revised and re-set several times before final approval.

After final approval of all aspects of the book you will refine and revise the specifications. It is time to mark up the manuscript and release it to the typesetter. This could take anywhere from a half day to as many as three days, depending upon the complexity and length of the book.

Marking up a book manuscript is as simple or as complex as the format demands. The important thing to remember is to keep it organized. You might try grouping the manuscript into three or four parts, such as: the front matter, consisting of the half title page, title page, copyright, dedication, table of contents and introduction; chapter openers; the actual text, separated into chapters; and the index. When writing the specs, it is not necessary to repeat them on every page if they are the same. Indicate what the requirements are on the first page of the text, for example, and state that they are to be followed throughout the attached 124 (or however many there are) manuscript pages. Of course you would review each page and mark up those portions that might vary from the overall specifications, such as indicating bold face, italics, certain indents, particular paragraph breaks, etc.

THE COMP ORDER SPEC SHEET

If the text contains several variations that are repeated it may be helpful to prepare a "spec sheet," better know as a "Comp Order," listing a series of coded specs to be followed so that all you need to do is label each portion of the text with a code letter or number.

While a coded spec sheet could save you a tremendous amount of mark up time, it could possibly become a burden to the typographer. Be careful not to overdo the coding, creating complicated spec sheets that go on for two or three pages. These instructions could become more difficult to follow than the job itself. It might be easier for the typesetter if you eliminate some of the coding specs and actually mark up the simple instructions such as bold face, space between groups, indents, etc. throughout the manuscript. It would also be helpful to provide him with type tissues, layouts or a dummy for further understanding of the job requirements. Fig. 73 is an example of a typical, simple spec sheet.

PREPARING A DUMMY

Whether you are speccing a manuscript for a book, booklet or brochure, the formula is very much the same and so is the mark up. The standard approach is to indicate the specs on the manuscript and have the type set in continuous galley form. On a lengthy manuscript it is advisable to order "readers proofs" rather than repros. Then, following your storyboard you can cut the galleys apart and prepare an actual size dummy layout, refining each page as you proceed, thus developing the final format and establishing a more precise number of pages.

This dummy can then be edited according to the needs and requirements of the project. Once final approval has been established, you can release either the edited dummy or a separate set of edited and revised readers proofs. You will then use the final repro proofs to prepare the mechanicals as per the dummy layout.

You will soon discover that once you have started cutting the readers galleys apart you can easily lose track of their sequence. This is obviously a critical aspect of the project and extreme measures should be taken to keep them in order. The editors proofread and mark up an extra set of galleys while the dummy book is used as a reference for position. Both the marked up galleys and dummy pages are sent back to the typesetter and must be coordinated in sequence. Of course you'll have an additional set of readers galleys for reference.

An accepted method used to keep it all together is to label each galley proof with a light color or yellow marker. This is done by writing the galley number directly on the proof in a step and repeat pattern. When the galleys are cut apart and pasted into the dummy the number or part of it will show; Fig. 74.

The approach just described is practical for a quick reference when working with a very large and/or involved manuscript. However, if the manuscript and book format are straight-forward, and few (if any) changes are anticipated, you can eliminate the dummy stage. Order repro proofs at the start and go directly to mechanicals, refining the layout as you go along. Revisions can then be done directly on the mechanicals. This does save time and money. It depends upon the nature and format of the book.

Another approach would be to prepare dummy pages. Make all the necessary layout revisions on the dummy and mark up any AA's on the corresponding duplicate galleys. Then have the typesetter revise the setting following the readers galleys and the dummy. The end result is a complete page make up by the typesetter which can be sent as negatives directly to the plate maker. This eliminates the need for mechnicals. It all depends upon the kind of equipment the typographer uses.

Fig. 73

Tom Cardamone Advertising Inc
16 East 52nd Street
New York, New York 10022
Telephone (212) 753-1356

DATE: December 4

JOB NUMBER: 1733

JOB TITLE: SCIENCE SUPPLEMENT
FRONT MATTER: TABLE OF CONTENTS and TEACHER'S NOTES

COMP ORDER FOR
SCIENCE SUPPLEMENT,
TABLE OF CONTENTS and TEACHER'S NOTES

(A) Headlines. 18 pt. MEMPHIS LIGHT with MEDIUM, all caps. Set in position with 1 pt. rules above and below, as shown on layout for TOC.

(TOC) 11/12 MELIOR with BOLD. Line for line, flush left. All 1 en space between numeral period and first word of text. Set in position as shown on layout for TOC.

(B) Subheads. 10 pt. MELIOR BOLD.

(C) Text Subheads. 8 pt. HELVETICA BOLD, c/lc.

(T) TEXT. 8/10 HELVETICA REGULAR. Flush left, rag right x maximum 19 picas.

(T-1) 8/9 HELVETICA REGULAR. Flush left, rag right x maximum 19 picas.

Fig. 74

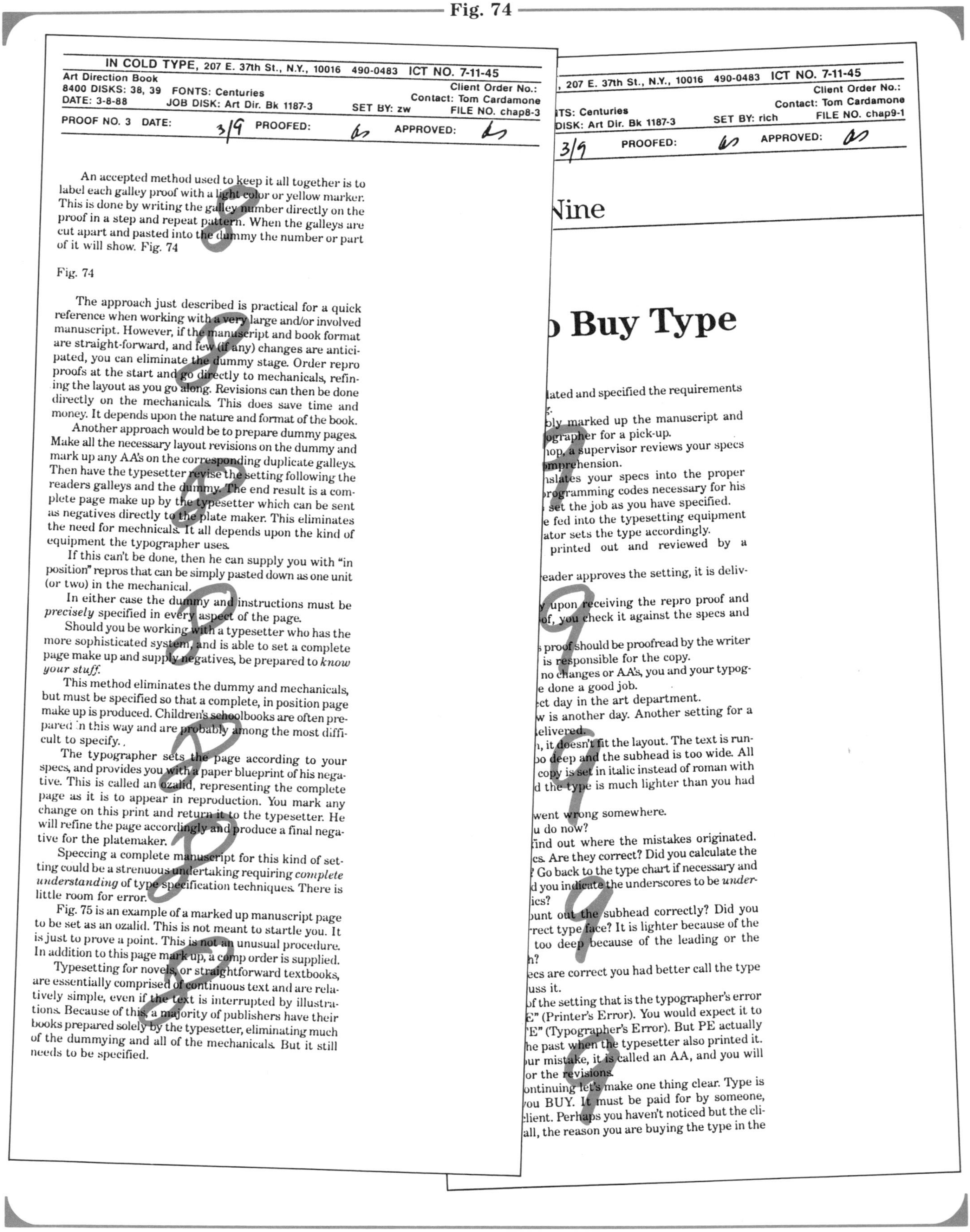

IN COLD TYPE, 207 E. 37th St., N.Y., 10016 490-0483 ICT NO. 7-11-45
Art Direction Book   Client Order No.:
8400 DISKS: 38, 39   FONTS: Centuries   Contact: Tom Cardamone
DATE: 3-8-88   JOB DISK: Art Dir. Bk 1187-3   SET BY: zw   FILE NO. chap8-3
PROOF NO. 3 DATE: 3/9 PROOFED: ___ APPROVED: ___

, 207 E. 37th St., N.Y., 10016 490-0483 ICT NO. 7-11-45
                                                      Client Order No.:
TS: Centuries   Contact: Tom Cardamone
DISK: Art Dir. Bk 1187-3   SET BY: rich   FILE NO. chap9-1
3/9   PROOFED: ___   APPROVED: ___

An accepted method used to keep it all together is to label each galley proof with a light color or yellow marker. This is done by writing the galley number directly on the proof in a step and repeat pattern. When the galleys are cut apart and pasted into the dummy the number or part of it will show. Fig. 74

Fig. 74

The approach just described is practical for a quick reference when working with a very large and/or involved manuscript. However, if the manuscript and book format are straight-forward, and few (if any) changes are anticipated, you can eliminate the dummy stage. Order repro proofs at the start and go directly to mechanicals, refining the layout as you go along. Revisions can then be done directly on the mechanicals. This does save time and money. It depends upon the nature and format of the book.

Another approach would be to prepare dummy pages. Make all the necessary layout revisions on the dummy and mark up any AA's on the corresponding duplicate galleys. Then have the typesetter revise the setting following the readers galleys and the dummy. The end result is a complete page make up by the typesetter which can be sent as negatives directly to the plate maker. This eliminates the need for mechnicals. It all depends upon the kind of equipment the typographer uses.

If this can't be done, then he can supply you with "in position" repros that can be simply pasted down as one unit (or two) in the mechanical.

In either case the dummy and instructions must be *precisely* specified in every aspect of the page.

Should you be working with a typesetter who has the more sophisticated system, and is able to set a complete page make up and supply negatives, be prepared to *know your stuff.*

This method eliminates the dummy and mechanicals, but must be specified so that a complete, in position page make up is produced. Children's schoolbooks are often prepared in this way and are probably among the most difficult to specify.

The typographer sets the page according to your specs, and provides you with a paper blueprint of his negative. This is called an ozalid, representing the complete page as it is to appear in reproduction. You mark any change on this print and return it to the typesetter. He will refine the page accordingly and produce a final negative for the platemaker.

Speccing a complete manuscript for this kind of setting could be a strenuous undertaking requiring *complete understanding* of type specification techniques. There is little room for error.

Fig. 75 is an example of a marked up manuscript page to be set as an ozalid. This is not meant to startle you. It is just to prove a point. This is not an unusual procedure. In addition to this page mark up, a comp order is supplied.

Typesetting for novels, or straightforward textbooks, are essentially comprised of continuous text and are relatively simple, even if the text is interrupted by illustrations. Because of this, a majority of publishers have their books prepared solely by the typesetter, eliminating much of the dummying and all of the mechanicals. But it still needs to be specified.

Nine

o Buy Type

lated and specified the requirements

bly marked up the manuscript and ographer for a pick-up.

hop, a supervisor reviews your specs omprehension.

nslates your specs into the proper rogramming codes necessary for his set the job as you have specified.

e fed into the typesetting equipment ator sets the type accordingly.

printed out and reviewed by a

eader approves the setting, it is deliv-

y upon receiving the repro proof and of, you check it against the specs and

s proof should be proofread by the writer is responsible for the copy.

no changes or AA's, you and your typog-e done a good job.

ct day in the art department.

w is another day. Another setting for a elivered.

h, it doesn't fit the layout. The text is run-o deep and the subhead is too wide. All copy is set in italic instead of roman with d the type is much lighter than you had

went wrong somewhere.

u do now?

ind out where the mistakes originated. s. Are they correct? Did you calculate the ? Go back to the type chart if necessary and d you indicate the underscores to be *under-*ics?

unt out the subhead correctly? Did you rrect type face? It is lighter because of the too deep because of the leading or the h?

es are correct you had better call the type uss it.

f the setting that is the typographer's error E" (Printer's Error). You would expect it to 'E" (Typographer's Error). But PE actually he past when the typesetter also printed it. ur mistake, it is called an AA, and you will or the revisions.

ontinuing let's make one thing clear. Type is ou BUY. It must be paid for by someone, lient. Perhaps you haven't noticed but the cli-all, the reason you are buying the type in the

─── **Fig. 75** ───

A nightmare

(NL) Name _____

(O) Study Skills: Test-taking Strategies

(P) Read each test direction and student answer. If the student
followed directions, cross out the words or phrases under the
box. If not, show the student's answer in the correct form.

1pt. ruled box 3 pi deep, width as indicated

 # to fill depth

1. Fill in the oval next to the word that completes each sentence.

18 pts. b/b
18 pts. rule to base
18 pts. base to rule
(FR)

In 1630, the Puritans formed a settlement called _____

18 pts. base to rule

⬭ Jamestown# ◯Plymouth# ◯ Massachusetts Bay #◯ Roanoke #

2½ pi
18 pts. rule to base
2½ pi

align ovals FL. LEFT

◯ Jamestown# ◯ Plymouth# ●Massachusetts Bay# ◯ Roanoke

2½ pi
27 pts. b/b   *2½ pi*   *answer - filled oval*

2. If a statement is ture, write True on the line ~~provided~~. If a
statement is false, write False.

18 pts. b/b
18 pts. base to rule
2½ pi

2½ pi

[T (FR) Roger Williams founded Rhode Island in 1635. [#]]

18 pts. rule to base
18 pts. base to rule

True Roger Williams founded Rhode Island in 1635.

27 pts. b/b
18 pts. rule to base
1pt. ruled box 3 pi deep, width as indicated

3. Circle the word that best completes each sentence.

18 pts. b/b

Anne Hutchinson and ~~her~~ followers built settlements that became ____. (FR)

2½ pi
18 pts. rule to base

18 pts. base to rule
2½ pi

#Connecticut# →New Hampshire# →(Massachusetts) #→Maryland#

rule through copy is answer — do not delete copy

FL. LEFT
2½ pi

Connecticut New Hampshire Massachuesetts Maryland

27 pts. b/b
18 pts. b/b

4. Answer each question with a complete sentence.

18 pts. b/b
18 pts. base to rule

What was the main cause for the settlement of Connecticut?

18 pts base to rule

27 pts

More Farmland

RRs × 28 pi
1 pi
18 pts

27pts

1 pi

_The main cause for the settlement of
Connecticut was the need for more farmland._

RRs × 28 pi

answer *27 pts. rule to base*

5. Write the correct ~~word~~ *answer* on the line.

18 pts. base to rule
2½ pi #

2½ pi

18 pts rule to base

#The first English settlement in America was called _____ . [#]

RR × 12 picas

18 pts. b/b *2½ pi*

Connecticut← →New Hampshire← (Jamestown)← →Roanoke[

18 pts. base to rule

18 pts. rule to base

The first English settlement in America was called _____ _Jamestown_ .

18 pts. b/b

Connecticut← →New Hampshire← →Jamestown← →Roanoke[

RR × 12 picas

#2½ pi

If this can't be done, then he can supply you with "in position" repros that can be simply pasted down as one unit (or two) in the mechanical.

In either case the dummy and instructions must be *precisely* specified in every aspect of the page.

Should you be working with a typesetter who has the more sophisticated system, and is able to set a complete page make up and supply negatives, be prepared to *know your stuff.*

This method eliminates the dummy and mechanicals, but must be specified so that a complete, in position page make up is produced. Children's schoolbooks are often prepared in this way and are probably among the most difficult to specify.

The typographer sets the page according to your specs, and provides you with a paper blueprint of his negative. This is called an ozalid, representing the complete page as it is to appear in reproduction. You mark any change on this print and return it to the typesetter. He will refine the page accordingly and produce a final negative for the platemaker.

Speccing a complete manuscript for this kind of setting could be a strenuous undertaking requiring *complete understanding* of type specification techniques. There is little room for error.

Fig. 75 is an example of a marked up manuscript page to be set as an ozalid. This is not meant to startle you. It is just to prove a point. This is an unusual procedure. In addition to this page mark up, a comp order is supplied.

Typesetting for novels, or straightforward textbooks, are essentially comprised of continuous text and are relatively simple, even if the text is interrupted by illustrations. Because of this, a majority of publishers have their books prepared solely by the typesetter, eliminating much of the dummying and all of the mechanicals. But it still needs to be specified.

Chapter Nine
Professionally Speaking

There is just so much one can learn by simply reading about a skill. The proof is in the doing. I cannot give you that experience but I will try to simulate it. The purpose of this chapter is to guide you through a complete project, step-by-step. Each aspect will be described as though you alone were actually doing the work, incorporating much of what has been described in previous chapters.

However, no terminology will be defined and no reason will be given for procedure. See if you can follow it with a complete understanding of the language. You might consider this exercise to be your first solo. . .

LET'S DO AN AD

You are the art director in a small ad agency and have been provided with the art, copy and layout requirements for a simple black and white ad. You have a tight deadline and a moderate budget, so the approach will be simple and direct.

The first thing you do is study the components that make up the ad. You have to incorporate the logo, headline, symbol, three product shots, copy, and ordering information. The ad is ½ page and measures 7⅛″ x 5″; Fig. 76.

You may want to sketch a few thumbnails to get the feel of the space and element relationship. Because there is not much room for creative design, your layout is going to be straightforward and organized; Fig. 77.

After your "warm up" sketches, you are satisfied that you can put it all together and sketch a layout actual size. At this point you are familiar enough with the elements to sketch them more closely to their relative proportion, simultaneously refining your layout; Fig. 78.

You are satisfied with your layout and feel you can "get it to work." You can at this time submit your rough sketch for approval before going into final production. However, this is a critical stage in the preparation of an ad.

Remember—you eyeballed the text. Should your layout be approved as it is and the type doesn't fit the way you designed it, you may have a serious problem getting it to look like your layout. You know this from experience. So it would be best to take it to the next phase before submitting it. You are going to prepare a slightly more comprehensive layout. In order to do this you must spec out the copy in anticipation of unforeseen space problems. This is also referred to as "casting off."

You flip through your type books in search of a headline face and jot down the names of those that appeal to you. Finally you have chosen Novarese Ultra for its style. However, you suspect that while it is a bold face it may not set dark enough on 30 picas to create the color you want. So, you'll have it condensed 20%. Rather than determining actual point size, you will have it set on the width. This will result in larger, darker letter forms within the same space, while the actual point size is arbitrary.

Fig. 76

D ECIDEDLY D EFINITELY D IGITAL

Logo

Symbol

c   MCA RECORDS

For mail order information contact:
Pack Central Inc.
6745 Denny Avenue
No.Hollywood, CA 91606

Product art

Copy

CONTINUING OUR TRADITION OF CLASSICAL & THEATRICAL RELEASES

FROM MCA'S LEGENDARY TAPE AND FILM VAULTS

2 COMPLETE CDS FOR THE PRICE OF 1 MIDLINE CD

BEETHOVEN		MCAD2-9809
DISC ONE	FIDELIO -- Act One Sena Jurinac . Jan Peerce Bavarian State Opera Chorus and Orchestra Hans Knappertsbusch: Conductor	
DISC TWO	FIDELIO -- Act One (Conclusion), Act Two . Sena Jurinac . Jan Peerce Bavarian State Opera Chorus and Orchestra Hans Knappertsbusch: Conductor	

BEETHOVEN		MCAD2-9810
DISC ONE	SYMPHONIES NOS.2 & 4 Pittsburgh Symphony Orchestra William Steinberg: Conductor	
DISC TWO	SYMPHONY NO.7 LEONORE OVERTURE NO.3 Pittsburgh Symphony Orchestra William Steinberg: Conductor	

WAGNER		MCAD2-9811
DISC ONE	OVERTURES: Rienzi . The Flying Dutchman Siegfried Idyll . Lohengrin Munich Philharmonic Orchestra Hans Knappertsbusch: Conductor	
DISC TWO	OVERTURES: Die Meistersinger . Tannhäuser Tristan und Isolde . Parsifal Munich Philharmonic Orchestra Hans Knappertsbusch: Conductor	

Also available: COPLAND: Billy the Kid/Rodeo/Appalachian
Spring/El Salon Mexico; GERSHWIN: Porgy & Bess/An American
in Paris/Piano Concerto in F. MCAD2-9800A/B • TCHAIKOVSKY:
Nutcracker Ballet (Complete);Swan Lake Ballet (Excerpts).
MCAD2-9801A/B • BEETHOVEN: Symphonies 1,3,6 and 8.
MCAD2-9802A/B • BEETHOVEN: Diabelli Variations/Sonatas 8,
14 and 23. MCAD2-9803A/B • BACH: St.John Passion. MCAD2-9804A/B •
BERLIOZ: Romeo & Juliet, Op.17/TCHAIKOVSKY: Romeo & Juliet
Fantasy-Overture. MCAD2-9805A/B • BEETHOVEN:Symphony No.9
in D Minor, Op.125 (Choral and Rehearsal Excerpts),
Symphony No.5 in C Minor, Op.67. MCAD2-9806A/B • VOISIN:
The Baroque Trumpet. MCAD2-9807A/B • MOZART: Symphonies 1-15.
MCAD2-9808A/B

— Fig. 77 —

— Fig. 78 —

MCClassics

DECIDEDLY **D**EFINITELY **D**IGITAL

CONTINUING OUR TRADITION OF CLASSICAL & THEATRICAL RELEASES

FROM MCA'S LEGENDARY TAPE AND FILM VAULTS   2 COMPLETE CDs FOR THE PRICE OF 1 MID LINE CD

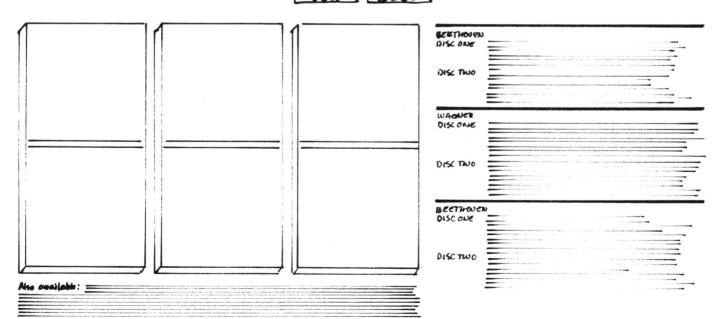

BEETHOVEN
DISC ONE

DISC TWO

WAGNER
DISC ONE

DISC TWO

BEETHOVEN
DISC ONE

DISC TWO

Also available:

For mail order information contact: Pack Central, Inc. 6745 Denny Avenue. No. Hollywood CA 91606   ©MCA RECORDS

In order to indicate the logo in position, you trace from a logo on file, or perhaps make a photocopy to size and paste it in position on the layout.

You now letter the headline, simulating the proper size and weight. This is not done as comprehensive lettering. A simple, single stroke letter with a pentel of the approximate weight is all that is necessary.

Then you sketch in the symbol and subhead, but feel that it needs a graphic device to hold it together, separating it from the main headline.

After having the product shots statted to size you tack them in position.

Now you have reached the challenging portion of the layout...the area to be occupied by the main text; Fig.79.

Copy A is to be set line for line as typed. The total count (including four rules) is 32. Using a shortcut to establish point size you place your type gauge over the text area and find the slot that shows 32 to be closest to the maximum depth; Fig. 80.

Seven point is smaller than you had anticipated but you have no choice unless you decide to change your layout. You check the chart for 7 point Triumvirate to see if it will fit on the *width*. "BEETHOVEN" measures 3.75 picas. "Bavarian State Opera Chorus and Orchestra" measures 11.50 picas. The total is 15.25 picas. The area you've designated measures 16.50 picas. So much for text A. You know it will fit.

Text B, however, is a bit more complicated, consisting of nine selections. It will have to be set so that each group is obvious. A square bullet between them may help, in addition to bold-facing the composer names and numbers. You also realize that hyphenations and bad line breaks are likely to occur if the type is set justified. Therefore, you have decided to set it flush left and rag right. For added clarity, it would be best to break each line after a selection, if possible.

The area you have to fit measures 25 x 3 picas. The box measures 25 picas leaving a maximum of 24 picas for the

---

Fig. 79

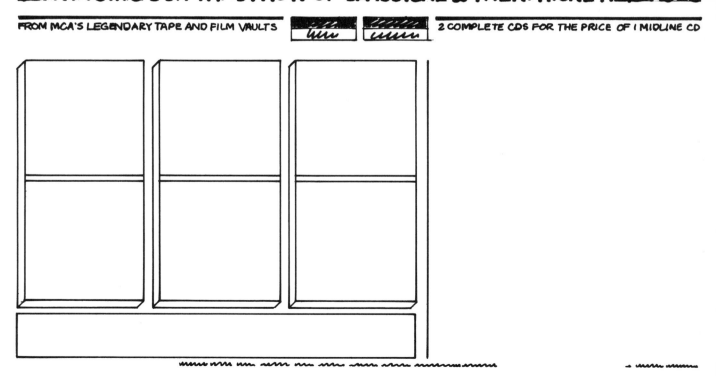

type. You have decided that 6 point Triumvirate Condensed with bold might fit. The type character count is 123.3 for a 24 pica line. But the text is heavily mixed with caps, lower case and numbers, making it difficult to get a workable character count. So you have decided to count and measure all the cap words separately from those that are upper and lower case.

The first group, ending after the first product number, consists of 131 lower case and 28 caps (including a one em space between the text and the bullet and one for the bullet). The calculation is as follows:

$$
\begin{array}{ll}
131 \text{ lc} & = 25.50 \text{ picas} \\
28 \text{ cps} & = \underline{\ \ 7.75} \text{ picas} \\
& \ 33.25 \text{ pica line length}
\end{array}
$$

This is entirely too wide and you really do not want to set it smaller. One thing you can do is shorten the count by placing "Also available" on a line by itself.

Your calculation now is:

$$
\begin{array}{ll}
115 \text{ lc} & = 22.50 \text{ picas} \\
28 \text{ cps} & = \underline{\ \ 7.75} \text{ picas} \\
& \ 30.25 \text{ picas}
\end{array}
$$

It is still too wide but you might be able to shorten the width of text A by setting it condensed. You'll check that later.

Using this first line as you guide (about 2.5 lines of typewritten text to one line of set type) you conclude it will run 7 lines deep (3.5 picas). Your layout is flexible enough to be revised to accommodate 3.5 picas. Now you recalculate the width of text A in 7 pt. condensed to determine whether you can use a 30.25 pica width:

$$
\begin{array}{ll}
9 \text{ bold cps condensed} & = 3.25 \\
41 \text{ lc condensed} & = \underline{\ 9.50} \\
& \ 12.75 \text{ pica width}
\end{array}
$$

Fig. 80

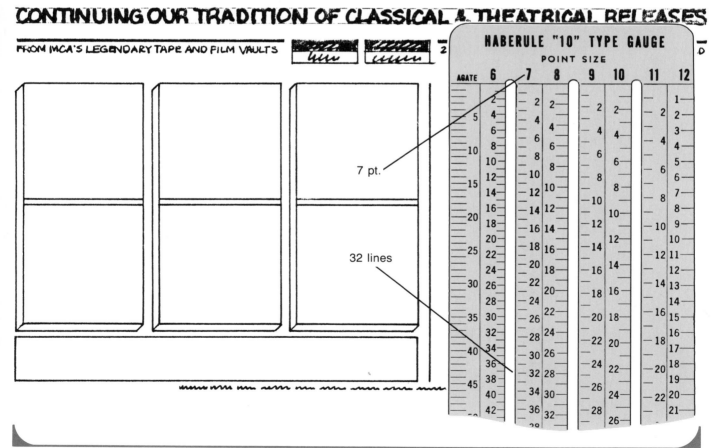

The overall width of the ad measures 43 picas. Your total calculation is: 12.75 (width of A) + 30 (width of B) = 42.75 picas.

You have calculated enough at this point to know that you will be able to get the layout to work with some adjustment. This is a critical part of any project. To continue calculating would be unnecessarily time consuming. You know when to stop because adjustments can be made during the mechanical preparation.

You are now ready to mark up the copy using the specifications you have developed; Fig. 81.

Fig. 81

Specced copy

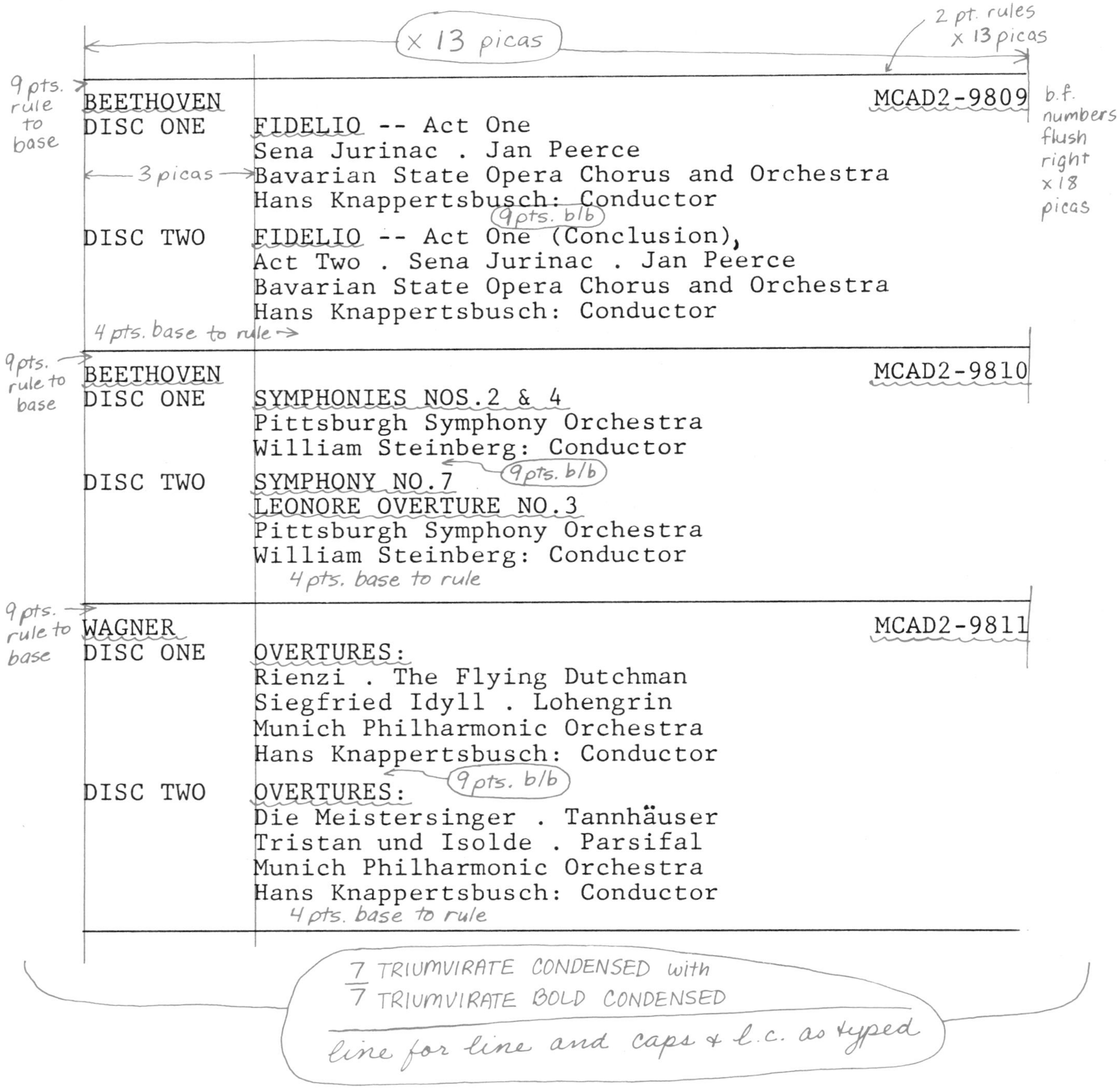

BEETHOVEN
DISC ONE   FIDELIO -- Act One
           Sena Jurinac . Jan Peerce
           Bavarian State Opera Chorus and Orchestra
           Hans Knappertsbusch: Conductor

DISC TWO   FIDELIO -- Act One (Conclusion),
           Act Two . Sena Jurinac . Jan Peerce
           Bavarian State Opera Chorus and Orchestra
           Hans Knappertsbusch: Conductor

MCAD2-9809

BEETHOVEN
DISC ONE   SYMPHONIES NOS.2 & 4
           Pittsburgh Symphony Orchestra
           William Steinberg: Conductor

DISC TWO   SYMPHONY NO.7
           LEONORE OVERTURE NO.3
           Pittsburgh Symphony Orchestra
           William Steinberg: Conductor

MCAD2-9810

WAGNER
DISC ONE   OVERTURES:
           Rienzi . The Flying Dutchman
           Siegfried Idyll . Lohengrin
           Munich Philharmonic Orchestra
           Hans Knappertsbusch: Conductor

DISC TWO   OVERTURES:
           Die Meistersinger . Tannhäuser
           Tristan und Isolde . Parsifal
           Munich Philharmonic Orchestra
           Hans Knappertsbusch: Conductor

MCAD2-9811

x 13 picas

2 pt. rules x 13 picas

9 pts. rule to base

3 picas

9 pts. b/b

b.f. numbers flush right x18 picas

4 pts. base to rule

9 pts. rule to base

9 pts. b/b

4 pts. base to rule

9 pts. rule to base

9 pts. b/b

4 pts. base to rule

7/7 TRIUMVIRATE CONDENSED with
TRIUMVIRATE BOLD CONDENSED
line for line and caps & l.c. as typed

Also available: COPLAND: Billy the Kid/Rodeo/Appalachian
Spring/El Salon Mexico; GERSHWIN: Porgy & Bess/An American
in Paris/Piano Concerto in F. MCAD2-9800A/B ■ TCHAIKOVSKY:
Nutcracker Ballet (Complete);Swan Lake Ballet (Excerpts).
MCAD2-9801A/B ■ BEETHOVEN: Symphonies 1,3,6 and 8.
MCAD2-9802A/B ■ BEETHOVEN: Diabelli Variations/Sonatas 8,
14 and 23. MCAD2-9803A/B ■ BACH: St.John Passion. MCAD2-9804A/B ■
BERLIOZ: Romeo & Juliet, Op.17/TCHAIKOVSKY: Romeo & Juliet
Fantasy-Overture. MCAD2-9805A/B ■ BEETHOVEN:Symphony No.9
in D Minor, Op.125 (Choral and Rehearsal Excerpts),
Symphony No.5 in C Minor, Op.67. MCAD2-9806A/B ■ VOISIN:
The Baroque Trumpet. MCAD2-9807A/B ■ MOZART: Symphonies 1-15.
MCAD2-9808A/B

6/6 TRIUMVIRATE CONDENSED with TRIUMVIRATE BOLD CONDENSED
7 lines flush left as broken
caps and c/lc as typed — use small, square bullets
between groups as indicated.

ITC NOVARESE ULTRA, ALL CAPS,
condense 20%. Set to 7⅛" on width.

CONTINUING OUR TRADITION OF CLASSICAL & THEATRICAL RELEASES

 # CUTTING
FROM MCA'S LEGENDARY TAPE AND FILM VAULTS
 # CUTTING
2 COMPLETE CDS FOR THE PRICE OF 1 MIDLINE CD

8 pt. TRIUMVIRATE BOLD
ALL CAPS

 # CUTTING

© MCA RECORDS   *6 pt. TRIUMVIRATE BOLD CONDENSED, caps*

 # CUTTING

For mail order information contact: Pack Central Inc.,
6745 Denny Avenue, No.Hollywood, CA 91606

7 pt.
TRIUMVIRATE
BOLD
CONDENSED,
1 line, c/lc

The repro shown in Fig. 82 is precisely as you specified. However, as you suspected, after carefully checking it against your layout, you see that some simple adjustments will have to be made.

- The headline is as you planned.
- You had calculated 17 picas for the subheads and they measure 16.5. You can stat them up but this size will be fine.
- The ordering information and copyright line will also fit.
- Text A is perfect as it is.

- Although Text B is legible it is a very tight setting and would have been easier to read had it been set with one point line spacing. If you had time you could call the type shop and have it opened. Under the circumstances you will have to use it as it is, but it is still too wide. You will have to reduce it from 30.75 picas to 28 making the type size 5½ point.
- The ad is finally mechanicalized; Fig. 83.
- You made your deadline.
- The client is pleased.

That's it.

Fig. 82

Type proof

CONTINUING OUR TRADITION OF CLASSICAL & THEATRICAL RELEASES

FROM MCA'S LEGENDARY TAPE AND FILM VAULTS

2 COMPLETE CDS FOR THE PRICE OF 1 MIDLINE CD

BEETHOVEN		**MCAD2-9809**
DISC ONE	**FIDELIO** — Act One	
	Sena Jurinac • Jan Peerce	
	Bavarian State Opera Chorus and Orchestra	
	Hans Knappertsbusch: Conductor	
DISC TWO	**FIDELIO** — Act One (Conclusion),	
	Act Two • Sena Jurinac • Jan Peerce	
	Bavarian State Opera Chorus and Orchestra	
	Hans Knappertsbusch: Conductor	

BEETHOVEN		**MCAD2-9810**
DISC ONE	**SYMPHONIES NOS. 2 & 4**	
	Pittsburgh Symphony Orchestra	
	William Steinberg: Conductor	
DISC TWO	**SYMPHONY NO. 7**	
	LEONORE OVERTURE NO. 3	
	Pittsburgh Symphony Orchestra	
	William Steinberg: Conductor	

WAGNER		**MCAD2-9811**
DISC ONE	**OVERTURES:**	
	Rienzi • The Flying Dutchman	
	Siegfried Idyll • Lohengrin	
	Munich Philharmonic Orchestra	
	Hans Knappertsbusch: Conductor	
DISC TWO	**OVERTURES:**	
	Die Meistersinger • Tannhäuser	
	Tristan und Isolde • Parsifal	
	Munich Philharmonic Orchestra	
	Hans Knappertsbusch: Conductor	

Also available:
COPLAND: Billy the Kid/Rodeo/Appalachian Spring/El Salon Mexico; **GERSHWIN:** Porgy & Bess/An American in Paris/Piano Concerto in F. **MCAD2-9800A/B** ■
TCHAIKOVSKY: Nutcracker Ballet (Complete); Swan Lake Ballet (Excerpts). **MCAD2-9801A/B** ■ **BEETHOVEN:** Symphonies 1, 3. 6, and 8. **MCAD2-9802A/B** ■
BEETHOVEN: Diabelli Variations/Sonatas 8, 14 and 23. **MCAD2-9803A/B** ■ **BACH:** St. John Passion. **MCAD2-9804A/B** ■
BERLIOZ: Romeo & Juliet, Op. 17/**TCHAIKOVSKY:** Romeo & Juliet Fantasy-Overture. **MCAD2-9805A/B** ■
BEETHOVEN: Symphony No. 9 in D Minor, Op. 125 (Choral and Rehearsal Excerpts), Symphony No. 5 in C Minor, Op. 67. **MCAD2-9806A/B** ■
VOISIN: The Baroque Trumpet. **MCAD2-9807A/B** ■ **MOZART:** Symphonies 1-15. **MCAD2-9808A/B**

© **MCA RECORDS**

For mail order information contact: Pack Central Inc., 6745 Denny Avenue, No. Hollywood, CA 91606

Your procedure may vary depending upon the complexity of the project. If you have the time and budget you can experiment with settings, or have the type shop solve a problem, allowing you the flexibility to make design decisions. This is not always possible. But your experience will enable you to apply your knowledge accordingly. While some projects may be simple, there are those that require much more than knowing how to count characters.

Fig. 83

Final Mechanical

CONTINUING OUR TRADITION OF CLASSICAL & THEATRICAL RELEASES

FROM MCA'S LEGENDARY TAPE AND FILM VAULTS royal blue double decker **2 COMPLETE CDS FOR THE PRICE OF 1 MIDLINE CD**

Also available:
COPLAND: Billy the Kid Rodeo Appalachian Spring El Salon Mexico. **GERSHWIN:** Porgy & Bess An American in Paris Piano Concerto in F. **MCAD2-9800A/B** ■
TCHAIKOVSKY: Nutcracker Ballet (Complete). Swan Lake Ballet (Excerpts). **MCAD2-9801A/B** ■ **BEETHOVEN:** Symphonies 1, 3, 6, and 8. **MCAD2-9802A/B** ■
BEETHOVEN: Diabelli Variations Sonatas 8, 14 and 23. **MCAD2-9803A/B** ■ **BACH:** St. John Passion. **MCAD2-9804A/B** ■
BERLIOZ: Romeo & Juliet, Op. 17 **TCHAIKOVSKY:** Romeo & Juliet Fantasy-Overture. **MCAD2-9805A/B** ■
BEETHOVEN: Symphony No. 9 in D Minor, Op. 125 (Choral and Rehearsal Excerpts). Symphony No. 5 in C Minor, Op. 67 **MCAD2-9806A/B** ■
VOISIN: The Baroque Trumpet. **MCAD2-9807A/B** ■ **MOZART:** Symphonies 1-15. **MCAD2-9808A/B** ■

BEETHOVEN		**MCAD2-9809**
DISC ONE	**FIDELIO** — Act One	
	Sena Jurinac • Jan Peerce	
	Bavarian State Opera Chorus and Orchestra	
	Hans Knappertsbusch: Conductor	
DISC TWO	**FIDELIO** — Act One (Conclusion),	
	Act Two • Sena Jurinac • Jan Peerce	
	Bavarian State Opera Chorus and Orchestra	
	Hans Knappertsbusch: Conductor	
BEETHOVEN		**MCAD2-9810**
DISC ONE	**SYMPHONIES NOS. 2 & 4**	
	Pittsburgh Symphony Orchestra	
	William Steinberg: Conductor	
DISC TWO	**SYMPHONY NO. 7**	
	LEONORE OVERTURE NO. 3	
	Pittsburgh Symphony Orchestra	
	William Steinberg: Conductor	
WAGNER		**MCAD2-9811**
DISC ONE	**OVERTURES:**	
	Rienzi • The Flying Dutchman	
	Siegfried Idyll • Lohengrin	
	Munich Philharmonic Orchestra	
	Hans Knappertsbusch: Conductor	
DISC TWO	**OVERTURES:**	
	Die Meistersinger • Tannhäuser	
	Tristan und Isolde • Parsifal	
	Munich Philharmonic Orchestra	
	Hans Knappertsbusch: Conductor	

For mail order information contact: Pack Central Inc., 6745 Denny Avenue, No. Hollywood, CA 91606 © **MCA RECORDS**

GENERAL REVIEW

The following illustrations represent several layout formats consisting of many standard configurations and their specification mark up. Study them as a general review and see how much of it you can understand. Actually you should be able to visualize all of it. If not...perhaps you need to go back a chapter or two or maybe review the symbols in chapter one. Remember, they make up the language of type speccing.

Furthermore, you might use this section as a reference if you have designed a format and are not certain how to mark it up. While your exact layout may not be shown here, perhaps it is composed of parts from more than one of these examples.

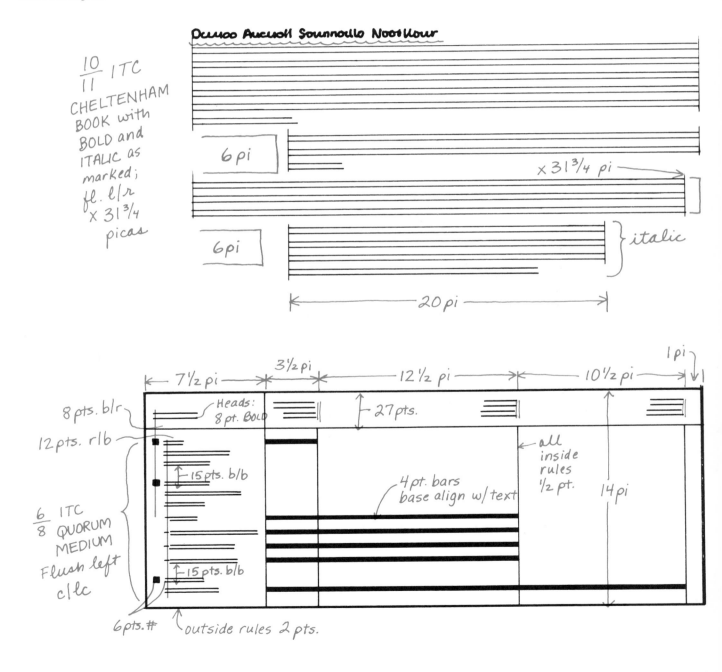

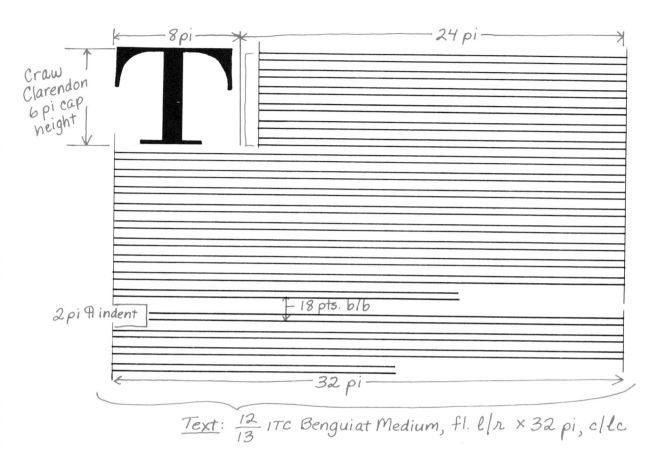

Text: $\frac{12}{13}$ ITC Benguiat Medium, fl. l/r × 32 pi, c/lc

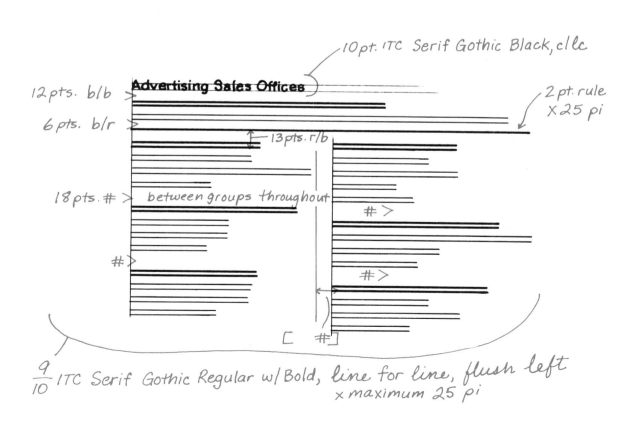

$\frac{9}{10}$ ITC Serif Gothic Regular w/ Bold, line for line, flush left
x maximum 25 pi

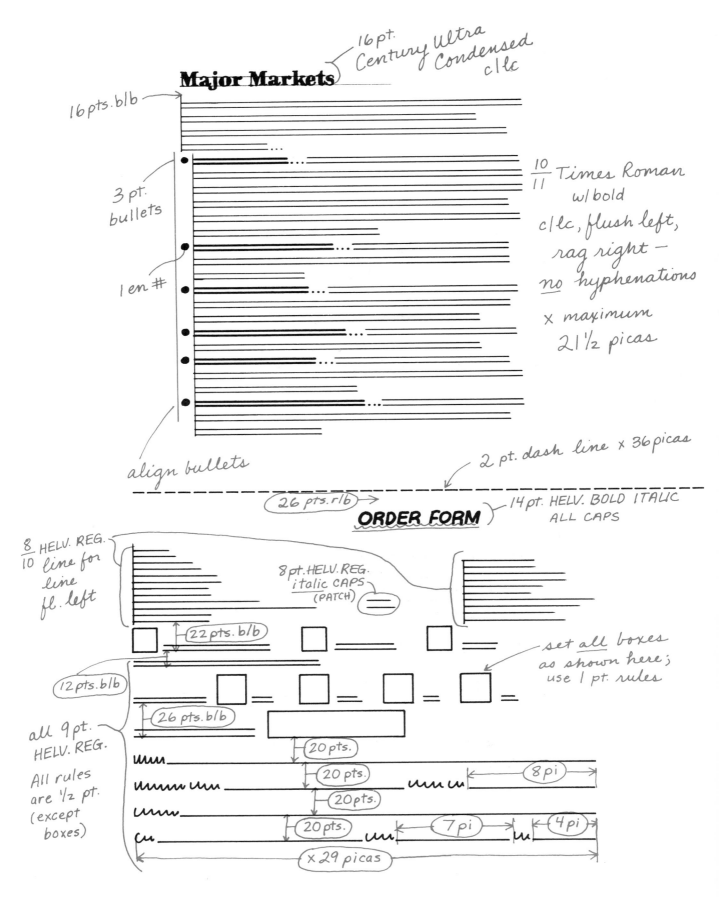

Major Markets

16 pt. Century Ultra Condensed c/lc

16 pts. b/b

3 pt. bullets

$\frac{10}{11}$ Times Roman w/ bold c/lc, flush left, rag right — no hyphenations

x maximum 21½ picas

1 en #

align bullets

2 pt. dash line x 36 picas

26 pts. r/b

ORDER FORM

14 pt. HELV. BOLD ITALIC ALL CAPS

$\frac{8}{10}$ HELV. REG. line for line fl. left

8 pt. HELV. REG. italic CAPS (PATCH)

22 pts. b/b

set all boxes as shown here; use 1 pt. rules

12 pts. b/b

all 9 pt. HELV. REG.

26 pts. b/b

All rules are ½ pt. (except boxes)

20 pts.

20 pts.

8 pi

20 pts.

7 pi   4 pi

20 pts.

x 29 picas

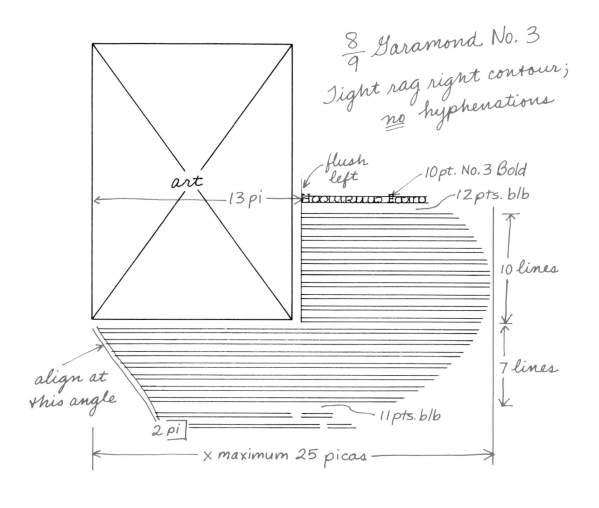

$\frac{8}{9}$ Garamond No. 3
Tight rag right contour;
<u>no</u> hyphenations

flush
left

10 pt. No. 3 Bold

12 pts. b/b

art

13 pi

10 lines

7 lines

align at
this angle

11 pts. b/b

2 pi

X maximum 25 picas

X 35 ¼ pi max

6 pts. to rule

5 pt. rule

24 pt.
Helvetica
Light

GROWTH

< #6 PTS. >

4 pi

Advertising pages:

[6 pi]

Year

[2
pi]

Pages

Year

[2
pi]

Pages

$\frac{10}{12}$ Helvetica Light w/ regular
flush right columns

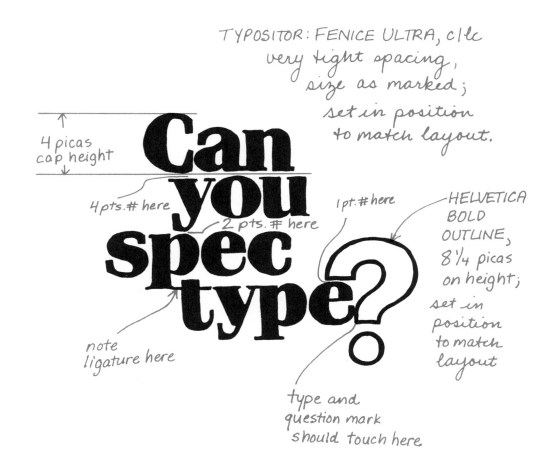

Chapter Ten

How To Buy Type

PROCEDURE

- You have calculated and specified the requirements of your setting.
- You have legibly marked up the manuscript and called the typographer for a pick-up.
- At the type shop, a supervisor reviews your specs for his own comprehension.
- He then translates your specs into the proper sequence of programming codes necessary for his typesetter to set the job as you have specified.
- The codes are fed into the typesetting equipment and the operator sets the type accordingly.
- A proof is printed out and reviewed by a proofreader.
- If the proofreader approves the setting, it is delivered to you.
- Immediately upon receiving the repro proof and reader's proof, you check it against the specs and layout.
- The reader's proof should be proofread by the editor or whoever is responsible for the copy.
- If there are no changes or AA's, you and your typographer have done a good job.

That's it! A perfect day in the art department.

But tomorrow is another day. Another setting for a different job is delivered.

To begin with, it doesn't fit the layout. The text is running four lines too deep and the subhead is too wide. All the underscored copy is set in italic instead of roman with underscores, and the type is much lighter than you had anticipated.

Something went wrong somewhere.

What do you do now?

Well, first find out where the mistakes originated. Check your specs. Are they correct? Did you calculate the depth properly? Go back to the type chart if necessary and check it out. Did you indicate the underscores to be *underscores*, not italics?

Did you count out the subhead correctly? Did you specify the correct type face? Is it lighter because of the leading? Is it too deep because of the leading or the size . . . or both?

If your specs are correct you had better call the type shop and discuss it.

Any part of the setting that is the typographer's error is called a "PE" (Printer's Error). You would expect it to be called a "TE" (Typographer's Error). But PE actually stems from the past when the typesetter also printed it.

If it is your mistake, it is called an AA, and you will be charged for the revisions.

Before continuing let's make one thing clear. Type is something you BUY. It must be paid for by someone, usually the client. Perhaps you haven't noticed but the client is, after all, the reason you are buying the type in the first place.

How can you avoid costly and time consuming problems? A few simple rules, mixed with some do's and don'ts, might be all you need.

THE PURCHASE ORDER

A purchase order can be as formal as required by the working arrangement between you and your typographer. While there is no definite format for a purchase order it should contain particular elements such as:

- The name, address and telephone number of your company
- Your name
- Specific job identification for billing purposes: i.e., the job number, title and name of client
- Billing instructions
- Delivery instructions
- Due time/date
- Material requested, i.e.:
    Number of reader's proofs (if any)
    Number of repros or print-outs

You will be charged for everything you order. So order only what you need. If two reader's proofs will be sufficient, be sure to indicate it on your order. Usually one print-out proof is standard while some shops provide two. If you want two or more, state it on your order.

Some of the top quality shops go one step further and prepare a "Diazo." This is a high quality repro proof printed on a better grade of paper. You are provided with a heavy weight glassene proof, two readers proofs and two repro proofs. The quality is top notch, the paper is easier to handle, you have an extra proof if needed and the advantage of the glassene for checking purposes. But weigh the facts before you order Diazos. They do cost more than the standard printout.

AUTHORS ALTERATIONS–REVISIONS– CHANGES–CORRECTIONS

Whatever you call it, it is the "magic word" when you receive the bill. More often than you may realize, the AA charges will be as much as, if not more than, the initial cost of a setting. In fact, AA's are so common in typesetting that ten or fifteen percent is usually added to a typesetting estimate.

What exactly is an AA? It is usually a change in the copy after it has been set. It could be as simple as inserting a comma or as involved as a complete copy change and resetting of a paragraph. Anything that is changed from the way it was in the original manuscript is an AA. It could also be a change in type face, type size, leading, measure, or deletion of copy. Regardless of what the change might be, you will be charged for it and most of all – it will take time.

There is no absolute way to avoid AA's but you can have some control over them.

Here are some guidelines that may be helpful:

- Know exactly what you want before you order it. In other words, take the time and make the effort to work out all the pertinent aspects of the setting.
- Avoid guessing when speccing. There is always the possibility that you are wrong. If, for some reason, you are uncertain about the type spec, call your typographer and discuss it.
- Avoid sending partial specs or partial manuscript. Try to order the entire setting at one time. The more often the typesetter has to "get back" to your job, the more it becomes time consuming and costly. If it isn't possible to order it at one time, be sure to indicate on your order "more to follow."
- On large, on-going projects be careful not to lose track of your specs. Develop a procedure to traffic the flow of proofs. Organize a system to avoid mixing galleys that are new vs. those that have been corrected, changed or billed. Color coding with markers is very helpful.
- Avoid a sloppy manuscript. Manuscripts that have been mutilated with handwritten edits, combined with complicated handwritten specs are often difficult to interpret. Use your judgment. If you can, have it retyped and rewrite your specs – legibly.
- If you are not sure that the copy will fit an area, or look esthetically pleasing, or whatever – order *reader's* proofs before going into final repros. You can use the reader's proofs to prepare a dummy layout in addition to having them proofread for AA's. Then, after everyone is satisfied with the setting, you can order the necessary changes and have repros set.
- When ordering simple AA's, you may save time by phoning them in. All the type proofs carry a code or identification of some sort. Refer to it when you call in the changes. If the AA's are extensive or complicated, it is best to mark them clearly on a reader's proof and have it picked up by the typesetter. It is advisable to indicate corrections clearly on an original reader's proof or copy of it. For example, if you have already prepared a mechanical and need changes, don't mark up the changes on a copy of the mechanical. Not having the code identification of the proof from which the mechanical was made makes it difficult for the typesetter to locate that portion of the copy on his equipment.

SET IN GALLERY

If you have repeat copy throughout a manuscript, such as a running foot or copyright line, it may be desirable to have it set on a separate galley. For example, a running foot might be copy that is repeated in the bottom margin of each of 40 pages in a book. Rather than have it set with the text for each page, have it set separately. But order it to be set 22 times and have two print-outs made. This way you will have your 40 settings (with 4 extras if needed). You simply type the copy *once* and mark it to be set 22 times in a column with cutting space between each line. This is common practice.

If you need folios (page numbers), order them the same way.

You can order corrections the same way if they are simple. It isn't necessary to reset an entire galley to correct a misspelled word or make punctuation changes. Maybe all you need to set is that particular line of copy or paragraph. These changes can be ganged up on one galley. Just indicate them as "patch corrections."

UP SIZE SETTINGS

On certain projects, such as in the preparation of artwork, the original may be created larger than the actual reproduction size. Usually one-half again the size (or one scaled up to one and one-half) also referred to as "half up" or focus 150%. That means that if labels or captions are required, the type must also be set "half up" so that when it is reduced to reproduction size it will be the correct size.

Type that is to print as 8 point will therefore be set in 12 point (half up from 8). When it is reduced (focus 66.6%) it will be 8 point.

Be advised that when choosing a type face for this kind of project, you ought to avoid delicate faces such as Bauer Bodoni, Devinne Italic or Helvetica Extra Light. They may not be strong enough to hold up through reduction, and might break.

THE REAL WORLD

Earlier in this book I mentioned that type specifying is a skill. The mathematics are simply a means of equating, your type specimen book is only a catalog of material, and the terminology and symbols are simply the means of communication. These are merely the tools and equipment you must use to perform the skill. You have yet to be confronted with their "real life" applications. The next step is to develop an in-depth understanding of the subject which can only be acquired through actual *on the job* experience. You need to get out there on your own. Make your own decisions. Form your own conclusions. Make your own mistakes. Enjoy the pleasure of your accomplishments.

Consider this text book an introduction to a valuable designer's tool. You have yet to use it to develop your own style. Your judgment, dictated by the requirements of a project, combined with your experience, are the major factors in determining procedure. In the final analysis, the most effective influence on a typesetting job is your ability to spec it.

Good luck.

The Text for this book was set by
Andy Guttentag and crew at
In Cold Type